We Just Build Hammers

Stories from the Past, Present, and Future of Responsible Tech

Coraline Ada Ehmke

Apress®

We Just Build Hammers: Stories from the Past, Present, and Future of Responsible Tech

Coraline Ada Ehmke
Chicago, IL, USA

ISBN-13 (pbk): 979-8-8688-1248-4   ISBN-13 (electronic): 979-8-8688-1249-1
https://doi.org/10.1007/979-8-8688-1249-1

Managing Director, Apress Media LLC: Welmoed Spahr
Acquisitions Editor: Shiva Ramachandran
Development Editor: James Markham
Project Manager: Jessica Vakili

Distributed to the book trade worldwide by Springer Science+Business Media New York, 1 New York Plaza, New York, NY 10004. Phone 1-800-SPRINGER, fax (201) 348-4505, e-mail orders-ny@springer-sbm.com, or visit www.springeronline.com. Apress Media, LLC is a California LLC and the sole member (owner) is Springer Science + Business Media Finance Inc (SSBM Finance Inc). SSBM Finance Inc is a **Delaware** corporation.

For information on translations, please e-mail booktranslations@springernature.com; for reprint, paperback, or audio rights, please e-mail bookpermissions@springernature.com.

Apress titles may be purchased in bulk for academic, corporate, or promotional use. eBook versions and licenses are also available for most titles. For more information, reference our Print and eBook Bulk Sales web page at http://www.apress.com/bulk-sales.

Table of Contents

About the Author

 **Coraline Ada Ehmke** is an internationally recognized tech ethicist, activist, and software engineer. For more than a decade, she has worked on practical approaches to promoting the values of diversity, equity, and justice in the technology industry. As a highly sought-after speaker, she has delivered keynotes at technology conferences on five continents.

She is best known as the creator of Contributor Covenant, the first and most widely adopted code of conduct for open source communities. She was recognized for her contributions to open source with a Ruby Hero Award in 2016. In 2018, she addressed the United Nations Forum on Business and Human Rights on the topic of human rights abuses by tech companies. In 2019, she authored the Hippocratic License, an innovative ethical source license tied to the United Nations Universal Declaration of Human Rights. She's profiled on Wikipedia where she is recognized as a pioneer among women in computing history. Her work has been featured by media outlets including CNN, the BBC, *WIRED*, *The Atlantic*, *The Wall Street Journal*, *The Guardian*, The Register, The Mary Sue, BuzzFeed, *Vice*, The Verge, ZDNet, The Daily Beast, and Business Insider.

Acknowledgments

Thank you to my partner Jess for everything, including teaching me that even writing a history book can be a creative practice. Thank you to my brother Aaz for being the very best rubber duck and accountability buddy I could ever ask for. Thanks to Matt, Crystal, Rynn, and the rest of the Lonely Hackers Club crew for all the virtual coworking and moral support. Thank you to Don for sticking with me and to Dave for believing in the project. And most of all, thanks to my daughter for always believing that her mom is a superhero whose power is caring about people.

Introduction

Speculative fiction gives us a chance to consider difficult ethical questions before we have to confront them in the real world.

Mary Wollstonecraft Shelley was 22 years old when she published ***Frankenstein; or, The Modern Prometheus***, in 1818. Her book was arguably the first work of speculative fiction in Western literature.

She grew up in the midst of the first Industrial Revolution, an age of tremendous social, technological, and economic change. Science and technology were making great advances, including breakthroughs in chemistry, biology, material science, metallurgy, and mechanical engineering. Production of goods requiring skilled handiwork was automated and industrialized. Mastery of steam power meant that machines could be operated with greater power and efficiency than ever before. Modern medicine introduced anesthesia, aspirin, vaccines, and the X-ray. With all of the rapid changes happening in the world, anything seemed possible, even harnessing the spark of life itself.

Frankenstein is a cautionary tale of the pursuit of scientific knowledge at all costs, unfettered by ethical constraints, and the complex and difficult relationship between the creator and the created. Frankenstein is less about the creature that young Victor galvanized into life and more about the psychic struggle and devastating, deadly consequences of his rejection of responsibility for his creation.

This book's fundamental question is, "Are we, as technologists, responsible for the technology that we bring into the world?" To arrive at our own answers to this question, we'll be using the lens of science fiction to explore the history and lineage of responsible tech.

Although I set out to write this book for my fellow technologists, I hope that it is accessible to a wider audience as well. After all, part of my core thesis is that technologists need to be in conversation with people outside of their own technological and cultural bubbles.

My generation of technologists, who came up in the 1990s, was raised to believe that the code we wrote was fundamentally neutral. We were building tools, like hammers. Sure, a hammer could be used to bash someone's skull, but it could also be used to build a house. It was really none of our concern. (We can blame a narrow reading of Noam Chomsky for reinforcing that particular idea.)

But over the course of my career, seeing the scale of the impact of even the most innocuous-seeming technologies on the world, I began questioning that fundamental belief. In the process, I've learned a lot about the world, a lot about my industry, and a lot about myself.

I wrote this book for people who would benefit from going on their own journey of ethical exploration and might want some guidance—and some company—along the way.

How This Book Is Organized

This book is divided into four parts, each corresponding to a different era of massive social and technological upheaval. Each part consists of three chapters. The first introduces an author or thinker who used speculative fiction to explore the question of the ethical obligations of technologists. Next, we meet the people who were influenced by their writing, directly or indirectly, and were inspired to factor social responsibility into their own work. The third chapter in each part describes what actually happened in the aftermath.

Part 1 deals with the Atomic Age. It introduces historian-of-the-future H.G. Wells and traces his influence on the Manhattan Project by way of real-life Martian physicist Leo Szilard.

Part 2 begins at the start of the nascent Digital Age, with computing pioneer Edmund Berkeley conceiving the personal computer, pondering mysterious strangers and unopenable safes, and fighting for his peers in the industry to consider their responsibility to society.

Part 3 explores the dystopian outlook of cyberpunk, its influence on the development of the hacker ethic, and the story of what happened when hackers started getting hired into big tech.

Part 4 traces New Wave science fiction's predictions about the intersection of technology and cultural conflict, how those predictions have been playing out since the 2010s, and what lies in store for responsible tech in the decades to come.

Let's Get Started

The question of our social responsibility as technologists is big and, honestly, scary. Luckily, we're not going on this journey alone. We're going to learn about a lineage of technologists *just like us* who wrestled with this same question over the past 100 years. We'll find out what strategies for making change worked and what didn't. We'll find inspiration in the stories and storytellers of our predecessors and, in the process, learn something deeper about our own relationship with our creations.

So keep an open and curious mind, and let's go on a journey through time together.

—Coraline Ada Ehmke, October 9, 2024

PART I

The World Set Free

CHAPTER 1

A Snare to Catch the Sun

The World Set Free, by futurist H.G. Wells, is a future history describing the political and social consequences of a world-changing discovery: the harnessing of atomic energy. Physicist Leo Szilard read the book in 1932 and, a year later, conceived the idea of neutron chain reactions. He assigned his patent to the British War Office to keep it safe from the wider scientific community, writing: "Knowing what this would mean—and I knew it because I had read H.G. Wells—I did not want this patent to become public." Szilard's ideas, and the warnings of Wells, were vital to the development of the atomic bomb during World War II, and especially to the subsequent efforts of scientists to mitigate the threat of global atomic warfare.

This chapter sets the stage for understanding the role of speculative fiction in shaping how we think about technology and responsibility.

The Future Starts Here

The Marconi Company achieves the first real-time transatlantic radio communication. Harry Brearley invents stainless steel in Sheffield, England. The Woolworth Building in New York City, designed by Cass Gilbert, rises to become the tallest building in the world.

© Coraline Ada Ehmke 2025
C. A. Ehmke, *We Just Build Hammers*, https://doi.org/10.1007/979-8-8688-1249-1_1

The value of world trade reaches nearly $40 billion. The Ford Motor Company builds the first automobile manufacturing factory to implement a moving assembly line. The Lincoln Highway is dedicated, the first road crossing the United States from coast to coast. Buenos Aires opens the first subway in the Southern Hemisphere.

Charles Fabry and Henri Buisson discover the ozone layer. William Temple Hornaday, a zoologist and one of the first wildlife conservationists, publishes **OUR VANISHING WILD LIFE**, cataloging for the first time endangered plant and animal species from around the world. Oskar Barnack invents the 35mm camera. Niels Bohr introduces the quantum model of the atom.

The year is 1913, and an amateur sociologist, teacher, and writer named Herbert George Wells has just published a "future history" called **THE WORLD SET FREE**. Wells's book is the first work of fiction to predict the atomic bomb and describes how the world might transform after this devastating technology is unleashed.

Wells was a pioneer in the emerging genre of speculative fiction. And as we will learn, speculative (or science) fiction has a long history of not just *foretelling* our futures, but actually *shaping* them—for better or for worse.

The Second Industrial Revolution

The world that Wells lived in was similar to today's world in some important ways.

The period between 1870 (soon after the end of the American Civil War) and 1914 (the start of World War I) is sometimes referred to as the Second Industrial Revolution. It was a time of massive social upheaval, driven by a combination of political, economic, and technological change. This era saw the rapid spread of industrialization, the triumph of the Protestant work ethic, and the birth of the millionaire industrialist class.

Advances in machinery and automation led to high demand for repetitive, "low-skill" labor in factories. Lines were blurred between factory and artisanal work. There were (often violent) conflicts over even basic labor rights in an increasingly automated world.

At the same time, private institutions were being modernized by fully embracing bureaucracy, causing a commensurate increase in demand for managerial and clerical positions.

Immigrants from around the world were drawn to the most industrialized countries by the promise of a better life, but often found themselves trapped at the very bottom of the increasingly divided social and economic strata.

Savvy industrialists drove a modernization of the class system, replacing the traditional European structure of "peasants, merchants, and nobles" with a virtuous hierarchy of "working, middle, and upper" classes. Separate pay systems were even put into place to emphasize the divide between clerical ("white-collar") and uniformed ("blue-collar") workers.

Through the realization of this fully modernized and rationalized socio-economic class system, business magnates managed to achieve equal status with the aristocracy of old Europe. This is not unlike how the billionaire class of today wields power and influence that even rivals that of most governments.

Introducing H.G. Wells

Herbert George Wells was born in Kent, England, in 1866, only a few short years before the start of the Second Industrial Revolution.

He was the fourth child of working-class parents. The family ran a small shop in Kent, but the business barely paid the bills and they relied on extra income from Wells's father's second career as a professional cricket player.

When an injury kept Joseph Wells from returning to the field, the family fell onto hard(er) times. His mother Sarah went to work as a domestic servant, and the three sons were sent into apprenticeships to help support the family. Later in his life, Wells would draw on memories of the atrocious working conditions he experienced to inform his theories of class and labor.

Wells was an avid reader and learner and convinced his parents to negotiate for an early end to his apprenticeship so that he could take a teaching position at a nearby grammar school. He continued his studies while he taught science and Latin and soon had the good fortune to win a scholarship to study biology in London.

He took an interest in writing and soon was selling articles and short, humorous works to London newspapers and periodicals. Wells began writing serialized stories that combined his passions for both science and literature. These "scientific romances," as they were called, were soon published as novels in their own right.

The success of the first of these novels, 1895's **THE TIME MACHINE**, confirmed his career prospects as a serious writer. The popularity of his subsequent novels, **THE INVISIBLE MAN** in 1897 and **WAR OF THE WORLDS** in 1898, freed him to focus on speculative fiction rather than journalism. (Later in his life, however, he quipped that he'd rather be remembered as a journalist than an artist.)

Wells was an incredibly prolific writer. Between 1895 and his death in 1946, he wrote 51 books and over 100 short stories. He saw his books banned and burned by Nazis in Berlin and praised for their genius in four nominations for the Nobel Prize for Literature. Through it all, Wells never let his literary success go to his head; he very deliberately and sincerely maintained the bearing and manner that befitted his roots as a working-class Englishman.

In September of 1936, almost exactly ten years before his death, Wells published his own imaginary obituary in the **NEW YORK TIMES**. It was a brilliant piece of good-natured self-deprecation, recounting his career as a "literary hack," his frequent bar brawls with fascists, and declaring poverty as the cause of his death at the age of 97.

Although much of his early work is firmly optimistic about the future of humanity, sometimes even utopian in its idealism, Wells grew more and more pessimistic as he watched two world wars unfold. In the preface for a 1940s reprinting of **THE WAR IN THE AIR**, one of his earlier works of militaristic science fiction, he declared that his tombstone would read, "I told you so, you damned fools!"

As he neared the end of his life, Wells experienced both the horror of seeing some of his predictions come true and the heartbreak of knowing that some of them never would. His final novel, **MIND AT THE END OF ITS TETHER**, grimly pits mankind against nature and posits the extinction of the species, told with an almost palpable sense of relief.

Wells was diabetic, and later in life, he suffered from heart problems and struggled with liver cancer. Despite his health problems, Wells lived to the age of 79, dying in London in August of 1946, one year after the end of World War II.

Today, Wells is best remembered for his works of speculative fiction, and in particular for their uncannily accurate predictions about the complex social and technological advances of the twentieth and twenty-first centuries. Given the similarities in the scope and scale of technological changes taking place in his world and ours, his work remains relevant and insightful.

The Politics of Peril

It seems to me that I am more to the Left than you, Mr. Stalin.

—H.G. Wells, **NEW STATESMAN**, October 27, 1934

Wells was prolific, but in many ways, the writing was simply a vehicle for his passionate political activism and uncompromising social criticism.

He was a fierce proponent of socialism, a member of the Fabian Society (a precursor to the liberal Labour Party in the United Kingdom), and even ran (unsuccessfully) for Parliament twice, in 1922 and 1923.

The early twentieth century saw a surge in radical right-wing ideologies, in particular nationalism, fascism, and antisemitism. Witnessing the rise of fascism throughout Europe in the 1920s and 1930s, Wells wrote two specifically antifascist novels.

First was **THE AUTOCRACY OF MR. PARHAM**, published in 1930, which follows the rise of a right-wing academic who, with the support of a corrupt millionaire industrialist, successfully overthrows the British government and initiates a disastrous second world war.

In 1939, he wrote **THE HOLY TERROR**, a complex political intrigue about the rise and fall of a Stalin-like, seemingly benevolent dictator whose political success eventually corrupts his idealism, turns him against his collaborators and allies, and inspires him to plot an anti-Jewish genocide.

While his antifascist novels attacked the rising popularity of right-wing ideologies and mocked its proponents through biting caricature, he was more direct in his criticism of real-world political leaders.

In pamphlets, articles, and newspaper interviews, he called Hitler an "unqualified horror" and "certifiable as a lunatic." He spoke of Mussolini's fatal vanity and described him as a "fantastic renegade from social democracy." Despite some early interest in the man and his political ideology, which he later disavowed, Wells criticized Stalin's "limited intelligence."

His frustration and alarm at the state of the world was not solely directed at overtly oppressive nationalist and fascist states. He was also a vocal critic of the British government, which he considered grossly incompetent in dealing with the rising crises spreading throughout Europe.

In the lead-up to World War II, Prime Minister Neville Chamberlain, a staunch Conservative, promoted a diplomatic policy of appeasement toward Hitler and Mussolini. Wells criticized Chamberlain as "ignorant, narrow-minded, and cowardly." He campaigned to support Winston Churchill to replace him as Prime Minister as war became clearly inevitable. Eventually, after the conclusion of World War II, Wells turned on Churchill as well, acknowledging that he had been an important symbol of British strength and resolve during the war, but had "outlived his usefulness."

Wells campaigned for broad reforms to social, economic, and military policies in the United Kingdom, the United States, and Australia. He believed that the United States held the best prospects for world peace, a perspective that he detailed in his book **THE FUTURE IN AMERICA: A SEARCH AFTER REALITIES**. In 1939, Wells declared that the United States was the "greatest hope for the salvation of mankind."

He was a great admirer of President Franklin D. Roosevelt, whom he visited in Washington several times. He was particularly intrigued by Roosevelt's so-called "Brains Trust," a circle of expert advisors drawn from academia, law, and economics. Wells referred to them as "social-minded technicians," but even his admiration for this group (and its fundamental multidisciplinary composition) did not exempt them from his criticism. To him, even the liberal policies of the New Deal did not go far enough.

The themes of Wells's writings were inherently and consistently political. Informed by his own experience and convictions, he promoted the view that, in light of the major social, political, and technological upheavals of the twentieth century, the future of the world itself was at stake: a position which, it could be argued, was not entirely unfounded.

A Search After Realities

We were making the future, but hardly any of us troubled to think what future we were making.

—H.G. Wells, **WHEN THE SLEEPER WAKES**

Throughout his writing, Wells made the case for a radical vision for the future. His nonfiction was analytical, persuasive, and intellectual, calling on readers to reflect critically on the present state of the world. His fiction was fantastical, scientific, and approachable, inviting readers to imagine alternative futures for the world.

Sometimes referred to as "Wells's Law," the fundamental rule that he followed in writing his "scientific romances" was that only one fantastical element was allowed per story. The narrative would depend on one novel fact being (or becoming) true: a vehicle capable of time travel is invented; a chemical compound is discovered that can turn a living thing invisible; an intelligent alien race possesses technology more advanced than our own.

What distinguished Wells's speculative fiction was that each of these single, fantastical ideas was placed in a domesticated context, to humanize it and to make it personal. He wanted it to be easy for his readers to imagine themselves as agents in his altered worlds. Readers would find themselves asking the question, "how would I feel if X were true, if X happened? What might happen to me as a result?"

By incorporating humanity into the futures his writing explored, he demonstrated his understanding of society as a techno-social system and helped people understand the potential consequences of major technological advances. He made scientific principles, both real and imagined, accessible to a wider readership. By engaging their imaginations and inviting them to place themselves in these alternate futures of utopia or dystopia, he appealed to a broader audience than his nonfiction prose attracted.

His writing demonstrated an understanding of how technological advancements could broaden or exaggerate existing social, economic, and political ills. His "future histories" held a magnifying glass to the flaws in modern society, flaws in modern institutions, and flaws in humanity itself.

In **THE TIME MACHINE**, the singular novel technology is a vehicle which enables time travel. The protagonist, a "gentleman scientist" in rural England, invents the machine and travels nearly a million years into a postapocalyptic future in which humanity has devolved into two extremes of being. One the one hand are the docile, almost childlike Eloi, living in a communist utopia, but constantly being preyed upon in the dark by creatures they are too frightened to even acknowledge. These are the pale, cannibalistic Morlocks, subterranean dwellers who both maintain the machinery that keeps the Eloi alive and also feed on their helpless wards. Through the fantastical vehicle of time travel, Wells is projecting his view of the increasingly stark class divisions of his time into a future where these divisions lead to an evolutionary bifurcation of humanity itself.

THE INVISIBLE MAN posits a chemical compound that can turn a living thing invisible. The protagonist, Griffin, invents this compound and applies it to himself, realizing too late that its effects are permanent. Leaving a wake of destruction behind him, he flees London for the countryside to work furiously toward a cure. Carefully covering his invisible body with clothes, gloves, and bandages, he presents himself to the townsfolk as a sort of "mysterious stranger." He tries to enlist and manipulate confederates to help him carry out a murderous and vengeful "reign of terror" across Britain. Although he's desperately seeking a way to reverse the chemical's effect on him, Griffin's plans also rely on his invisibility to escape the consequences of his actions. He is essentially using science as a cover to enable him to act immorally and with complete impunity.

In **WAR OF THE WORLDS**, Wells imagines an alien race on Mars hungrily eyeing the plenitude of natural resources on their neighbor, Earth. The Martians launch a military assault upon an unsuspecting planet, wielding overwhelmingly superior technology capable of reducing human civilization to ruin. **WAR OF THE WORLDS** was inspired in part by the genocide British invaders committed against indigenous Tasmanians in the "Black War" of the early nineteenth century. The novel reflects the immorality of British imperialism back on itself, projecting its plunderous history of colonialism through an image of relentless alien invasion of Britain itself.

Wells was not alone in using fiction to critique the state of the world, but his fiction was unique in its interweaving of the physical and social sciences. His future histories were a lens for exploring the role of technology in contemporary social and political contexts. By placing futuristic technologies in prosaic settings, he entertained his readers while subtly subverting their assumptions and perceptions of the modern world. With the sleight of hand of a single disruptive technological truth, his stories drew lines connecting present conflicts to fantastical yet plausible futures.

From our modern perspective, we can understand Wells as a sort of propagandist for futurology, an author of techno-social parables. His nonfiction keenly described the world as it was; his fiction compellingly explored the world as it could be.

Through both his fiction and nonfiction, Wells emphasized the two ingredients he considered essential to the survival of the human race: the globalization of governance, and the responsible application of new technologies.

Toward a Scientific Global Order

In his formative years, Wells experienced firsthand the consequences that came with the reordering of the socio-economic class system during the Second Industrial Revolution. His later formal education in the sciences tempered and refined his understanding of these experiences and inspired his particular approach to mapping out paths to alternative futures.

Wells believed that the world needed a new social order, informed by science: an alternative to the current system that was imposed by capitalism. Throughout his life, he persistently made the case, in works of fiction and nonfiction, for a new approach to governance that surpassed the unending, increasingly bloody conflicts between nation-states, and "treated the world as a single problem."

Wells asserted that the survival of human civilization depended on a scientific ordering of society, at a global scale. For example, in **THE WORLD SET FREE**, he writes:

> *The council was gathered together with the haste of a salvage expedition—the only possibilities of the case were either the relapse of mankind to the agricultural barbarism from which it had emerged so painfully, or the acceptance of achieved science as the basis of a new social order.*

The future society that Wells imagined was not simply a rearrangement of social systems in response to scientific advances, but rather the application of scientific principles and methodologies in the design and structure of social systems themselves. The science that Wells was advocating was the emerging science of sociology.

Wells engaged with sociology primarily through an interest in the design and critique of utopian social systems. He believed that such systems could benefit from gains in productivity, efficiency, and industriousness that would come from successive technological revolutions. A utopian socialist society would provide solutions to the "social contradictions" and moral poverty of capitalism, using technology to move humanity toward greater freedom and equity and away from precarity and scarcity.

The world was shrinking, making the need for international cooperation and unity increasingly urgent. Wells consistently stressed the necessity of global collaboration in light of increasingly devastating military power. He saw that with each major technological advance, our capacity for destruction only grew.

Wells's conception of political and social order was most clearly laid out in his 1940 book **THE NEW WORLD ORDER**. In this book, he explored the philosophy of structural functionalism, in which political authority is organized into international agencies with responsibility for shared needs and shared functions. In the system he described, political organization would be horizontal, rather than hierarchical; collectivist, rather than individualist; and would prioritize social and ethical concerns over unfettered technological advancement.

Most importantly, Wells saw how the perverse incentives of capitalism and the irrational decisions of its institutions restrained the practice of creativity. His emergence as an influential and prolific literary figure gave him the freedom, credibility, and audience to imagine alternate futures "out loud," in the hope of inspiring new generations of scientists, philosophers, and artists to do the same.

Wells As Techno-optimist

A frequent theme of Wells's work was the mastery of power through technological advances. His concept of power was not purely industrial, but rather human industriousness itself. It is a power that arises from and sustains civilization. In his estimation, the evolution of humankind was inseparable from the evolution of human technology.

Wells's early writings, in the 1890s, exhibited what scholar Bernard Bergonzi described as "a kind of fatalistic pessimism, combined with intellectual skepticism." Bergonzi noted that the anticipation of the turning of the nineteenth to twentieth century made such existential angst commonplace—not unlike the turning of the twentieth to twenty-first century.

In the years between 1900 and the start of World War I, Wells's estimation of the prospects of humanity slowly began to improve, and he became a sort of evangelist for a philosophy that today we call techno-optimism.

Techno-optimism is the belief that technology has the potential to improve the lives and circumstances of people around the world. While the promise of such a future resonated with his utopian yearnings, Wells retained enough of his skepticism to understand that the opposite was equally possible: that emerging technologies could spark our descent into a dystopian future.

Wells understood that revolutions in technology could have psychological, social, and political impact out of proportion to their scientific impact. In his optimistic moods, Wells invoked future histories of a world where mastery of technology freed its citizens from toil. In his darker moods, he fantasized about how the fatal flaws in our characters might leverage those technologies to bring about the end of civilization itself.

Inductive History

And the question arises how far this absolute ignorance of the future is a fixed and necessary condition of human life, and how far some application of intellectual methods may not attenuate even if it does not absolutely set aside the veil between ourselves and things to come. And I am venturing to suggest to you that along certain lines and with certain qualifications and limitations a working knowledge of things in the future is a possible and practicable thing.

—H.G. Wells, **THE DISCOVERY OF THE FUTURE**

Wells was uncomfortable with the idea that the future of humanity might be left to its irrational and often self-destructive impulses. He set out to develop a methodology for studying potential futures and the forces that might bring about (or prevent) them. It was a sort of rational futurology that he called "inductive history," essentially applying the methodologies of social sciences to chart paths to alternate possible futures.

Throughout the nineteenth century and into the first few decades of the twentieth, the philosophical underpinnings of sociology as a scientific discipline weren't yet completely settled. Conflicting theories of social science struggled to take hold in a world transformed by a quick succession of social, technological, political, and scientific upheavals.

The particular current of social science that Wells subscribed to sought to apply rationality to the problems of ethics and morality. Its proponents held that the goal of sociology should be the rational reform of politics, economics, and society in general. Wells saw this as a necessary antidote to the irrationality that made our human future so precarious.

His case for inductive history was most clearly laid out in a lecture that he gave to the Royal Institution in 1902 titled "The Discovery of the Future." In this lecture, Wells posited that there were two types of minds: "legal minds" that focused on the past and "creative minds" that focused on the future. The former were traditionalists who used the past to justify the conditions of the present: "Things have been, says the legal mind, and so we are here." The latter were revolutionaries who attacked and sought to alter the status quo: "We are here because things have yet to be."

Wells saw inductive history as a way to identify potential futures, and reveal the rational decisions that would guide civilization from *here* to *there*. Just as geology and archaeology allow us to visualize the past almost as clearly as the present, he hoped that inductive history would allow us to see the future with just as much clarity. This hypothesis is even hinted at in the title of his lecture. The future would not be predicted, so much as discovered.

The Science of Future History

By the turn of the twentieth century, there was widespread belief that human progress relied upon a steady progression of scientific knowledge and technological innovation. This embrace of scientific advancement made the emerging genre of speculative fiction particularly compelling and lent credibility to Wells's literary interrogations of possible futures.

On a Saturday night in November 1933, as part of a series of programs commemorating its tenth anniversary, the BBC broadcast an address by Wells titled "Wanted: Professors of Foresight!" The **RADIO TIMES** synopsis of the program promised that Wells would provide a "characteristically provocative answer" to the question of where accelerating scientific progress would lead us.

In the broadcast, Wells used the example of the motor car to highlight how little foresight is applied to anticipating the consequences of technological advancements. He pointed out how obvious it should have been that automobiles would radically change roads, the transport of passengers and goods, and even the distribution of the population. Yet, no preparations for these changes were made.

His frustration was evident. "We have let consequence after consequence take us by surprise," he said. "It is only after something has hit us hard that we set about dealing with it."

To address this widespread lack of forward-looking planning, Wells called for an entirely new field of study and practice, which he dubbed "Foresight." This new science would be devoted to anticipating the social, cultural, and political impact of new technologies. Noting that there were thousands of academics studying history, he exclaimed, "There is not a single Professor of Foresight in the world; but why shouldn't there be?"

A year later, in 1933, a report titled "Recent Social Trends in the United States" was published by a special committee commissioned by President Herbert Hoover. The committee's charter was to study changes in demographic, educational, and cultural aspects of American society. At the beginning of the report, a note explained that the researchers had strategically chosen or excluded certain lines of inquiry, for example, "the fateful issue of war and peace" or "the growth of scientific knowledge in general," in their analysis and projections. The publication of this report is considered to be the first milestone in the emerging science of futurology.

The term "futurology" itself was coined some years later by Ossip Flechtheim, a political scientist who fled Nazi Germany in 1935. In his writing, he echoed Wells's call to establish the study of the future as a serious field of scientific and academic research. Flechtheim envisioned futurology as a radical means of understanding human society "in the hitherto forbidden future tense."

In 1944, US Army General Henry Arnold tasked Hungarian-American mathematician and physicist Dr. Theodore von Kármán with establishing a group of scientists to evaluate the aeronautical research and development capabilities of the Axis powers. Based on this evaluation, the Scientific Advisory Group of the United States Air Force was to recommend future areas of research for the Air Force's own R&D programs. In effect, they were prioritizing research according to the probability of different technological advances occurring.

This new science of the future was deeply influenced by speculative fiction. Today, what practitioners call "futures studies" is an interdisciplinary field that examines past and present social, technological, and environmental trends to extrapolate possible futures. There is an emphasis on a plurality of futures: some preferable, some undesirable; some plausible, some unlikely.

Wells's future histories shined a light on what was possible and gave people permission to imagine alternate futures. But he insisted on the need for rational approaches for bringing these futures about or averting their catastrophe. As he wrote in **The Discovery of the Future**, "the imagination, unless it is strengthened by a very sound training in the laws of causation, wanders like a lost child in the blankness of things to come and returns empty."

A Prophetic Trilogy

The world went about its business [...] just as though the possible was impossible, as though the inevitable was postponed for ever.

—H.G. Wells, **THE WORLD SET FREE**

In 1913, H.G. Wells wrote one of his most influential future histories, titled **THE WORLD SET FREE: A PROPHETIC TRILOGY**. In the book, Wells described a future in which humanity would develop atomic weapons and bring about a devastating global war. Ultimately, humanity came to its senses and created a peaceful world society, by harnessing the atom as an energy source rather than an instrument of destruction.

Like much of his writing, **THE WORLD SET FREE** first appeared in serialized form, this time in the venerable **CENTURY**, an illustrated monthly magazine published in New York. The magazine was a major influence on leading figures in politics, society, religion, and art. For decades, **CENTURY** was the highest-selling illustrated periodical in the United States and boasted contributions from the likes of Nikola Tesla, Booker T. Washington, Jack London, W.E.B. DuBois, and even future president Theodore Roosevelt. (When **THE WORLD SET FREE** was published in 1914, the magazine's editor was Robert Underwood Johnson, whose earlier career had earned him recognition as "the father of international copyright law.")

The scientific basis of **THE WORLD SET FREE** was informed by Wells's readings in contemporary physics and chemistry, in particular the work of William Ramsay, Ernest Rutherford, and Frederick Soddy.

William Ramsay was a Scottish chemist and Nobel Prize winner who had identified an entirely new class of elements known as the "noble gasses," including the isolation of neon, krypton, xenon, and argon. Ramsay had also collaborated with British chemist Emily Aston in developing techniques for measuring atomic weight.

19

Ernest Rutherford, a physicist from New Zealand, was dubbed the "father of nuclear physics" for his many scientific discoveries, including the half-life of radioactive elements, radon as the sixth noble gas, and the existence of neutrons. Much of his work, specifically around artificially induced nuclear reactions and transmutation, built on Marie Curie's theories of radioactivity. Rutherford would famously oversee the series of experiments by his students Cockrof and Walton that resulted in the splitting of an atom.

Frederick Soddy was an English scientist, Nobel Prize winner, and pioneer in the field of radioactive chemistry. Soddy's achievements included his work with collaborator Ada Hitchins leading to the discovery of the radioactive disintegration of uranium. Soddy was specifically recognized and honored by Wells: **THE WORLD SET FREE** was dedicated to Soddy's 1909 **INTERPRETATION OF RADIUM**. (Soddy returned the honor by praising Wells in **WEALTH, VIRTUAL WEALTH, AND DEBT**, a book that proved influential in the later development of ecological economics.)

Ramsay, Rutherford, and Soddy all shared the opinion that, even though nuclear reactions and radioactive decay released energy, atomic energy had no real potential as a practical source of power. Rutherford had even declared that "anyone who looked for a source of power in the transformation of the atoms was talking moonshine." This was the consensus of the scientific community at large. Nobel Prize–winning physicist Robert Millikan, addressing the Society of Arts and Sciences in 1929, assured his audience that there was no reason to "dread the day when some unscrupulous Dr. Faustus may [use atomic energy to] blow this comfortable world of ours into star-dust."

The World at War

Never before in the history of warfare had there been such a weapon. These atomic bombs which science burst upon the world that night were strange even to the men who made them.

—H.G. Wells, **THE WORLD SET FREE**

The central premise of **THE WORLD SET FREE**, the singular novel technological fact upon which the story relies, is simply that Ramsay, Rutherford, Soddy, and their contemporaries were wrong about the world-changing implications of atomic energy.

Wells tells the story of a fictional scientist named Holsten, who as a child prodigy gained fame as an extraordinary mathematician. Inspired by his study of the luminescence of fireflies and the gift of a "little scientific toy," Holsten engaged in research that eventually disproved Ramsay, Rutherford, and Soddy (who were called out by name in the text), solving what scientists insisted was an intractable problem through a "wonderful combination of induction, intuition, and luck." By 1933, Holsten had demonstrated how splitting the atom could, in fact, produce immense energy. And, as Wells applied his inductive history to project what would happen in the real world under these circumstances, the immense power of atomic energy was first used for military advantage.

In the midst of global labor unrest, literal architectural stratification by social class, and the flight of competent men from public and political affairs, the military powers of the world were free to obsess over "rearranging the maps" of Europe and the larger globe. Inevitably, infected with the "outworn tradition [...] of sovereign states," the world plunges into total war.

Wells describes the response of the Allied forces to the destruction of their headquarters in Paris by German forces. Their response is to launch a single, low-flying aircraft equipped to fly to Berlin under cover of a cloudy night sky and throw down upon the city three atomic bombs in a gleeful act of vengeance.

21

The bombs were thrown by hand by a bombardier in the open-cockpit, helicopter-like aircraft. Ignition of the spherical, two-handled bomb was initiated by biting through a plastic stud protruding from a black, carolinium sphere. Thus ignited, the bomb was then quickly thrown at the target below. The force of its initial explosion drove the bomb several feet below the surface of the ground, then created a massive explosion that made the area of impact resemble the crater of an active volcano. A roiling, seemingly perpetual firestorm swirled from the crater, spewing radioactive waves of energy that slowly receded over a 17-day half-life. Berlin lay in ruins, and the forces of the Central European states were defeated.

A New World Order

Wells was excited by the potential benefits of technology, but was also acutely aware of its dark side, how easily it could be weaponized. And he saw very clearly that, in the twentieth century, global war was the inevitable result of modern nationalist states. The introduction of atomic energy in a world so divided could very well bring about the total collapse of human civilization.

Wells's own conviction about the necessity of world government is presented in his novel as the solution to the existential threat of atomic warfare. Humanity must finally shrug off the "carnivorous ghosts" of the empires of Greece and Rome, the "disordered thoughts and violent impulses" of nation-states, in favor of an equitable, rational, scientific world government.

Of the novel's architects of this new world order, he writes, "From the first they had to see the round globe as one problem; it was impossible any longer to deal with it piece by piece. They had to secure it universally from any fresh outbreak of atomic destruction, and they had to ensure a permanent and universal pacification."

Harnessing atomic energy as an abundant, limitless energy source would bring about this lasting peace and promote the well-being of every person on earth. "The bulk of activity in the world no longer lies with necessities," the narrator reflects. "The majority of our population now consists of artists and poets."

Reflection

Science fiction scholar and anthologist James Gunn characterizes much of Wells's work as "propaganda novels that resemble science fiction."

The alternately bright and dark threads of his predictions, warnings, and promises were woven into the fabric of his fiction and his nonfiction. His novels sought to make the fundamentals of his worldview relatable, and his nonfiction sought to make them practicable. Often he seemed to explore his own ideas first through the lens of his fiction, then allow the prophecies of the narrative to inform their design and constraints. This interplay of fiction and nonfiction was, in fact, the fundamental machinery of his inductive futurology.

"As a matter of fact," Wells proclaimed in an address to the Royal Institution of London, "prophecy has always been inseparably associated with the idea of scientific research."

This chapter took us back in time to the Second Industrial Revolution, introduced H.G. Wells and his work, and gave us our first taste of speculative fiction as a history of the future. Next, we'll see how Well's writing influenced a certain Hungarian physicist whose work proved critical to harnessing the power of the atom.

CHAPTER 2

The War to End All Wars

H.G. Wells was witness to a wave of incredible scientific progress that swept across the Western world in the 1920s and 1930s, and the fear and wonder of the age is reflected in his writing. During this time, new fields of research emerged. Novel methods of experimentation were developed. Long-entrenched theories about the workings of the universe were scrutinized, disproved, rejected. Mathematics, chemistry, and physics were being reinvented daily. What had once seemed impossible, now became imaginable. Science seemed ready to propel humanity toward a more hopeful future.

But the political order of Europe, which had never quite recovered from World War I, overshadowed this future. Fascists and nationalists took power in Germany, Italy, Spain, Greece, and Portugal and were met with an attitude of appeasement, or even a covert sympathy, by their neighboring countries, whose objective was to stave off a second world war at all costs.

In this chapter, we'll see how the entanglement of these powerful forces, at this particular moment in time, foregrounded science for politicians and politics for scientists.

© Coraline Ada Ehmke 2025
C. A. Ehmke, *We Just Build Hammers*, https://doi.org/10.1007/979-8-8688-1249-1_2

Introducing Leo Szilard

Two brothers sat in a small salon in a cramped four-room apartment, just a few blocks from the Technical Institute of Berlin where both were studying. A handwritten sign on the wall by the door declared, "Friendly Invitations to Stay Longer Should Not Be Taken at Face Value."

The brothers were frequently visited by fellow students seeking help with their coursework, and today, one such student sat on the edge of a chair in the salon, explaining his difficulties. The younger brother, Bela, listened intently, while the older brother, Leo, sat in his chair, silently staring into space, apparently lost in a daydream. But as Bela responded to the young man's questions, Leo grew more and more impatient with the conversation and with his brother for indulging the boy.

Abruptly, Leo sat bolt upright, fixed his gaze on the young man, and demanded: "Question: what is an optimist?" A beat later, before the startled student could reply, Leo barked, "Answer: one who thinks that the future is uncertain."

This was a question that Leo Szilard often put to strangers and new acquaintances alike. He had a mind that could find unexpected connections between systems, facts, theories, and paradoxes alike. Problems that were considered intractable by the scientific establishment became puzzles for him. He considered the impossible an almost personal challenge to his powers of logic, rationality, and imagination.

Szilard in Hungary

Leo Szilard, born to a Hungarian Jewish family, began his studies in 1916 at the Palatine Joseph Technical University, in his native city of Budapest. He fell in love with physics during his early school years, but was discouraged from pursuing the field because of its dismal career prospects. His second choice, chemistry, also promised very little in the way of employment. Finally, he resigned himself to studying civil and mechanical engineering.

But only a year after entering the University, Szilard found his academic career abruptly put on hold. At the start of World War I, he was pressed into compulsory military service. He served a relatively uneventful term of enlistment as an officer in the Austro-Hungarian Army and was discharged in 1918 following its defeat.

Hungary changed over the course of the war. It lost its status as one of the most powerful kingdoms in Europe, along with much of its prewar territory and nearly two-thirds of its civilian population after borders were redrawn. Amid feelings of humiliation at its losses, conflict between various ethnic groups who blamed each other for Hungary's defeat led to wide-ranging political instability.

Despite this political unrest, the Szilard brothers did their best to return to the normalcy of the civilian lives they had led in Budapest before the war.

Back at the university, Szilard briefly became active in the socialist student movement. His political worldview attempted to reconcile socialism with his innate rationalism. Szilard was certain that it was possible to solve social, political, and economic problems using pure reason.

He attended impromptu meetings at the nearby New York Café, a famous gathering place where students, artists, and political activists engaged in impassioned debate. Here, Szilard earned something of a reputation for his lack of diplomacy, if not outright rudeness, and his tendency toward arguing as a "devil's advocate."

He was quick to call out inconsistencies or irrationalities that he perceived in the viewpoints of his fellow students in the movement. He sometimes brought conversations to a halt to demand explanations of fundamental economic or political concepts that he could not rationalize.

His impatience with the irrationality of politics, and his frustration with socialist policies that he considered too simplistic to be practicable, alienated Szilard from many of his fellow activists. Politics, it seemed, brought with it problems that one could not simply sit in a bath and solve from first principles. Nonetheless, he went on to make an entire second career of trying to do just that: to reshape political and economic realities to conform to rational principles.

Soon, the internecine and largely ethnic conflicts within Hungary gave rise to an increasingly authoritarian government. This nationalist backlash brought with it a rising anti-Semitic sentiment. Szilard's family, like many other Jewish families, attempted to avoid scrutiny and further assimilate by converting from Judaism to Calvinism.

But Szilard and his brother Bela still found themselves increasingly ostracized and imperiled because of their Jewish heritage. By the autumn of 1919, almost a year after the end of World War I, they were once again prevented from pursuing their studies. A crowd of students at the gates of the university barred their entry, threatening them with violence and shouting anti-Semitic abuse. The brothers even came under formal investigation by government authorities for their political activities.

It was clear that Budapest was no longer safe. Szilard unsuccessfully tried to convince his friends, family, and peers to flee Hungary, but most of those he spoke to were resistant to the idea and felt that he was making the political situation seem more dire than it really was. Finally, after desperately calling in family favors, bribing indifferent officials, and enlisting the aid of sympathetic professors, Szilard managed to leave his native Hungary to live and study in Berlin.

The Berlin Years

I only want to know the facts of physics. I will make up the theories myself.

—Leo Szilard, 1920

Like his native Hungary, Germany also suffered economically and politically from its defeat in the war. But to Szilard, Berlin still seemed safer than Budapest and offered him some hope for a future.

Perhaps the strongest draw for Szilard was that Berlin was the de facto center for scientific research in Europe. Before and after World War I, prominent institutions in Berlin maintained strong connections with other scientific hubs throughout the continent. Conferences in the city drew prominent scientists from all over the world, creating opportunities for collaboration across disciplines and borders.

Berlin's thriving scientific community was home to influential physicists, mathematicians, and other scientists. Szilard began attending lectures, first at the Institute for Technology, then at the Kaiser Wilhelm Institute. Inspired by the spirit of scientific revolution he felt all around him, he decided at last to devote himself to physics after all. (He later quipped that Budapest had been the perfect place for budding physicists to begin their studies, because the instructors were so incompetent they had to learn to teach themselves.)

Szilard was welcomed into a community of teachers and mentors, friends, and friendly adversaries. He began to truly thrive, intellectually and socially. He benefited from the culture of wild conjecture, passionate debate, interdisciplinary collaboration, and unbounded imagination that spanned Berlin's laboratories, lecture halls, and coffee shops. He moved in scientific circles that included past and future Nobel laureates and other preeminent figures, including John von Neumann, Otto Hahn, Werner Heisenberg, and Lise Meitner.

His academic work focused on physics and mathematics, and he attended lectures by the likes of Einstein and Planck. But his interests were broad, and Szilard also deeply studied philosophy and ethics. He found himself particularly drawn to the Rationalism of Descartes, Spinoza, Leibniz, and Kant.

Rationalism is a philosophy that posits the existence of universal truths that transcend our ability to perceive them. These truths can be discovered by reasoning alone, rather than empirical observation or evidence. Szilard likely found this philosophy particularly validating given his typical approach to problem-solving: episodes of what he called "botching," which involved spending long hours in a hot bath, deep in thought about some problem or question.

Szilard's formal education culminated in a PhD in 1922. His doctoral dissertation presented a solution to the paradox of Maxwell's demon. Maxwell's demon was a famous thought experiment that seemed to challenge fundamental principles in thermodynamics, and had long been considered unsolvable. Einstein, to whom Szilard first presented his solution, was astonished. "It's impossible. This is something that cannot be done," he said. Szilard's reply was, "Yes, but I did it."

Over the next decade, Szilard continued to make important contributions to the fields of quantum physics, thermodynamics, and mathematics and even coinvented, with Einstein, a new kind of refrigerator with no moving parts. His thesis and subsequent research and experimentation led to radical new theories about information and entropy, which decades later influenced the development of information theory as a new field of human endeavor.

Fleeing Germany

Germany's economy could not keep pace with its debts, which totaled nearly 130 billion marks (approximately $30 billion 2024 US dollars). The German mark was losing value exponentially, rendering the currency all but worthless.

Economic instability led to political instability, and soon, Berlin's scientific preeminence was overshadowed by dire political developments, culminating in the ascension of Hitler and his Nazi regime in 1933.

Soon, book bonfires devoured the work of thinkers like Einstein, Wells, Proust, and Sinclair, among others. Scientific progress in Germany was thrown into chaos, as new laws removed hundreds of intellectuals, scientists, and academics, especially those of Jewish heritage, from their positions. The revolutionary scientific developments of Berlin's heyday, including quantum physics and the theory of relativity, were dismissed by the Nazis as part of a conspiratorial "Jewish world-bluff."

Szilard was certain that a second world war in Europe was imminent, and he began planning his escape. Once again, he found himself urging friends and colleagues in Germany, and his family in Hungary, to flee while they still could. Many other scientists, including Einstein, Fermi, Bohr, Franck, and Wigner, were also working to escape Nazi Germany and seek refuge abroad.

Szilard left Berlin on March 30, 1933, with two suitcases in hand, on a train bound for Vienna. He managed to scrounge up enough money for a first-class ticket, in the hopes that it would help him avoid scrutiny at the German-Czech border. In fact, the scheme worked.

The following day, the same train line from Berlin to Vienna was crowded with would-be refugees fleeing the Nazis. But before the train was allowed to leave the station, Nazi troopers moved through the cars, removing any "non-Aryan" passengers from the train and seizing their belongings.

Reflecting on his lucky escape some years later, Szilard said, "if you want to survive in this world you don't have to be much cleverer than other people; you just have to be one day earlier."

The Scientific Diaspora

Once in Vienna, Szilard connected with his friend Hermann Franz Mark. Mark had been part of the scientific circles in Berlin and had even collaborated with Einstein on X-ray experiments to help the physicist test some of his new theories of quantum physics.

After earning his PhD, Mark took a position as head of research and development at the German chemical conglomerate IG Farben, which at the time was the largest corporation in Europe and the fourth-largest in the world.

During his decade at IG Farben, Mark pioneered the science of polymers, a technology that soon drew the attention of the Third Reich. As the political situation in Germany continued to deteriorate, a colleague advised Mark to return to his native Vienna while he still could.

The company he left behind attracted Hitler's favor. The Third Reich began investing heavily in IG Farben, and its industrial research capabilities became crucial to the German war effort. (After World War II, the company was discovered to have used slave labor, provided by nearby concentration camps, in its manufacturing facilities. Its executives plead ignorance.)

Szilard knew that his own escape had been lucky and feared for the safety of his many friends and colleagues who were left behind. Even as the danger steadily increased through the 1930s, there was little or no money or effort put toward rescuing persecuted scientists and academics.

Szilard and Mark were united in their concern and decided to work together to address the refugee crisis. They tapped into their respective professional networks to find sympathetic peers they hoped could help. Szilard even traveled back and forth to London, where he and Sir William Beveridge of the London School of Economics cofounded the Academic Assistance Council. This organization helped more than 2,000 refugees escape to Britain, the United States, and Canada just ahead of the start of World War II.

Among the scientists who fled during this time was a contingent of Hungarian scientists of Jewish heritage, who jokingly referred to themselves as "the Martians." Their "secret" was that they had actually come from another planet to assist the Allies in the fight against fascism. They spoke Hungarian to disguise their extraterrestrial origin and to explain away their awkwardness in adapting to life in their adoptive countries.

This group included mathematician John Von Neumann, recognized as the father of the modern computer; Eugene Wigner, considered the first nuclear engineer; Theodore von Kármán, a pioneering figure in aeronautics; Edward Teller, who gained infamy for his role in developing the hydrogen bomb in the 1950s; and of course, Szilard himself.

A Subatomic Puzzle

Even as the threat against Szilard and his peers was rising and Europe was tilting rapidly into fascism, scientific progress continued.

In January of 1932, Irène Joliot-Curie and her husband Frédéric Joliot-Curie conducted a series of experiments investigating the properties of an atom's nucleus. Their latest experiment was intended to detect positrons, a theoretical subatomic particle that was the antimatter equivalent to the electron. If they could prove the existence of the positron, the couple could settle a long-standing and hotly debated problem essential to reconciling certain theories of quantum mechanics.

They conducted this experiment by bombarding a quantity of polonium, a very rare and very unstable radioactive metal, with gamma rays. Their precious sample of polonium had been passed down to Irène by her mother, Marie Skłodowska-Curie, whose pioneering work on radioactivity made her the first woman recognized with a Nobel Prize. Iréne hoped that the success of the positron experiment would finally earn her a place of honor next to her mother in the history of physics.

Their experiment was a success, but tragically, the couple misinterpreted their results and considered it a failure. Suspecting that the Curies may have made a mistake, other physicists sought to quietly reproduce and reinterpret their results.

James Chadwick, an English physicist who had worked under the supervision of Ernest Rutherford, was one of these scientists. He used a sample of polonium sent from Germany by his friend Lise Meitner and built an experimental apparatus to help prove the theory of the neutron. Another physicist, Carl David Anderson, conducted similar experiments but substituted thallium for polonium and soon confirmed the proof of the positron's existence.

Chadwick was credited with the discovery of the neutron, Anderson for the discovery of the positron, and both men were later awarded Nobel Prizes for their work. (The Curies were awarded their own Nobel Prize a few years later, in 1935, in acknowledgment of their pioneering work on artificially inducing radioactivity.)

The Secret Patents

Knowing what this [a neutron chain reaction] would mean— and I knew it because I had read HG Wells—I did not want this patent to become public.

—Leo Szilard

In 1933, one year after Chadwick and Anderson published their results, Szilard stood at a busy intersection, waiting for a traffic light to change, and had an epiphany: it should be possible to take advantage of neutrons to set off a self-perpetuating series of atomic reactions that could generate tremendous amounts of energy seemingly out of nowhere. Szilard had, very suddenly and very unexpectedly, conceived the idea of a neutron chain reaction.

Szilard filed for patents based on his neutron chain reaction idea in 1934. One set of patents involved simple atomic reactions involving single neutrons, which he considered important but relatively innocuous. The second set of patents described the more complex, and literally explosive, chain reaction concept.

He had read H.G. Wells's **THE WORLD SET FREE** the year before and certainly had the writer's depiction of the devastating possibility of atomic warfare in mind as he struggled with what to do with his idea. Given the state of the world and his belief that a second world war was imminent, Szilard feared the consequences should the idea of the neutron chain reaction come to the attention of the Germans or other Axis powers. Somehow, the chain reaction patents would have to be safely and secretly tucked away.

He decided to offer the patents to the British War Office, asking in return that they be marked classified and kept safe. But Szilard floundered trying to convince them that his patents were worth protecting. They seemed impractical for either civilian or military use, and his intentions were suspect. However, his persistence eventually paid off, and it was the Admiralty of the British Navy that finally confirmed a classified seal on the patents in 1936.

Szilard had done his best to keep the idea of neutron chain reactions under a veil of secrecy, safe from those who might abuse it. Now, he just had to prove that his theory was correct.

Impositions

In so far as the present discoveries in physics are concerned, the forecast of the writers may prove to be more accurate than the forecast of the scientists.

—Leo Szilard, in a 1934 letter to Hugo Hirst, founder of General Electric UK

Szilard spent the next few years in London, uncertain about how to proceed. He desperately needed to find a position, either in academia or in private industry, that would grant him the autonomy, budget, and suitably equipped laboratory he needed to continue his research into neutron chain reactions.

35

He managed occasional trips from London to Chicago and New York to visit his peers, with or without invitation. He enjoyed haunting their labs, peering over the shoulders of the lab workers, even interrupting the work from time to time to ask maddening series of questions. This was his way of keeping up with the scientific progress being made by other physicists.

He may also have believed that, by virtue of his presence and persistence, a colleague might be moved to invite him to stay.

Although he was too proud to explicitly ask them for help, many of his friends and colleagues went out of their way to recommend Szilard to prominent universities in England, Canada, and the United States. But his very precise and expensive requirements, and perhaps his awkward and grating way of communicating, ruined his chances for most of these opportunities.

With his academic prospects dwindling, Szilard attempted to secure funding from private interests. If his theories on nuclear chain reactions were correct, the possibilities for its peacetime, domestic use were immense.

Through a mutual contact, he connected with Hugo Hirst, founder of General Electric (UK), and C. C. Paterson, the company's director of research and development. Szilard hoped that with their support, he could conduct the research and experimentation needed to prove his theories.

But Szilard refused to do more than hint about the nature of his theories to his would-be investors. He promised that given complete discretion and sufficient time and money, he would bring them a technology that would radically transform energy and industry. But Szilard's awkwardness and refusal to provide specific details failed to earn the trust of the GE executives.

In March of 1934, Einstein helped his friend Szilard secure a grant from the Rockefeller Foundation that allowed him to pursue his research at New York University. Even with this temporary appointment, he managed to irritate his hosts, insisting on splitting his time between New York and Europe. Some of his colleagues began to joke about his trick of being in two places at once.

Frustrated by the lack of investment by either academic or industrial institutions, Szilard decided to try a different approach. He managed to make an interesting arrangement with the administration of St Bartholomew's, an ancient and well-regarded teaching hospital in London. He worked in the physics lab on medical applications of current advances in physics and chemistry. Through this work, he developed techniques for using radioactive isotopes as a diagnostic tool that are still in use today. In exchange, the director of the physics department allowed him to use the hospital's laboratory during the summer holidays, accompanied by an assistant chosen by the director.

But after years of trying, Szilard was still unable to prove his theory of nuclear chain reactions. On December 19, 1938, he resignedly wrote a letter to the British Admiralty, apologizing for wasting their time and rescinding his request to keep his (apparently useless) patents classified.

Fact or Fission

All the things which HG Wells had predicted appeared suddenly real to me.

—Leo Szilard

It was on the same day that Szilard sent his regretful letter that his former colleagues Otto Hahn and Fritz Strassmann split the atom. The pair had remained in Berlin and continued their work at the Kaiser Wilhelm Institute even after Szilard, Lise Meitner, and many other of their peers had fled Germany.

Hahn and Strassmann's experiment involved firing neutrons at a uranium nucleus. They were able to detect the presence of barium in the resulting atomic debris, which at first they could not understand: how could a mere neutron cause a heavy uranium nucleus to break apart and transmute? Frustrated, Hahn wrote to Meitner, who had taken a safe but unsatisfactory position at the Nobel Institute for Physics in Stockholm. His letter asked for her help in understanding their experimental results.

Meitner's nephew Otto Frisch, himself a physicist, happened to be visiting her from Denmark over the winter break. After reading the letter together, Meitner and Frisch took a walk in the woods to talk through the problem that Hahn presented.

Taking a break at a snowy tree stump, the spark of an idea formed. Meitner began performing mental calculations while Frisch drew explanatory diagrams in the snow, and soon, a theory emerged that could explain what they called the "fission" of the uranium nucleus. Their theory not only explained the presence of barium in Hahn's experiment, but was also validated by Einstein's theory of relativity.

Meitner excitedly wrote back to her friend to tell him about the new theory and immediately submitted a paper, titled "Disintegration of Uranium by Neutrons: a New Type of Nuclear Reaction," to the journal **NATURE**. Hahn and Strassmann separately submitted their own research to the journal **NATURWISSENSCHAFTEN** ("The Science of Nature"), failing to credit Meitner and Frisch. The Hahn and Strassmann paper made it to print first, and Hahn was later awarded a Nobel Prize for the work. Meitner and Frisch's paper was printed a month later, in early February of 1939.

When news of the discovery of uranium fission reached Szilard in New York, he realized that his theory had now, finally, been proven true. Uranium was the key element required for a neutron chain reaction, not indium or beryllium as he previously believed.

Armed with this new understanding, Szilard was eager to begin experimenting with uranium fission. While Fermi had been engaged for some time in separate research on neutrons, Szilard was able to convince his Columbia University colleague that the fission work was more important: the published science now made a fission-based "super bomb" a possibility.

On March 3, Szilard and Fermi carried out an experiment that connected Szilard's theories with the fission results and proved that successive fissions released more energy in the form of neutrons. The neutron chain reaction was real.

"We turned the switch, saw the flashes, watched for ten minutes, then switched everything off and went home," Szilard later reflected. "That night I knew the world was headed for sorrow."

Forestalling the Foretold

I am quite aware that the view which I am taking on the subject may be very exaggerated. Nevertheless, the feeling that I must not publish anything which might spread information of this kind indiscriminately has so far prevented me from publishing anything on this subject.

—Leo Szilard

Leo Szilard was sure that, given the implications of the neutron chain reaction theory, the safest thing to do was to keep the discovery secret, to prevent nations like Germany from using their work to produce their own atomic weapons. Fermi, on the other hand, believed that transparency, not secrecy, was the most conservative approach. At the time, he did not share Szilard's belief in either the peacetime or wartime utility of atomic energy.

Since his flight from Berlin in 1933, Szilard had been sure that a second war with Germany was inevitable. Szilard tried to convince his colleagues around the world to stop publishing their findings on nuclear physics, but such an idea stood at odds with the widely held, orthodox belief in science as the apolitical pursuit of "knowledge for knowledge's sake."

Very few people in scientific or political circles seemed to understand or care about the dangers that might lay ahead. The Joliot-Curies at least believed in the threat of Nazi Germany harnessing atomic energy and hid away all of their research on nuclear fission under the protection of the French Academy of Sciences.

Nevertheless, by the end of 1939, the possibility of harnessing atomic power through nuclear chain reactions was openly discussed in the newspapers and journals of the day, but not treated with the expected seriousness that was warranted. On his popular radio show, comedian Fred Allen joked that splitting the atom only made sense if someone came into a science lab one day "and wanted half an atom." Newsweek recalled remarks that Einstein had made years before, along the lines that pursuing atomic energy was as useless as "shooting birds in the dark." Some newspapers criticized fantasists like H.G. Wells for fanning the flames and playing up the imaginary danger of atomic weaponry.

Most physicists still agreed that the practical application of atomic energy was at best a remote possibility. The simple fact of uranium's scarcity, and the difficulty of purifying it at large scale, seemed to support their position.

At the time, the largest reserves of uranium were in Czechoslovakia in Europe and the Congo in Africa. Czechoslovakia was annexed by Germany in 1938, and the Congo was under Belgian colonial control. When Germany invaded Belgium in 1940 and immediately stopped the country's sale of uranium, Szilard's fears of a looming Nazi nuclear weapons program suddenly seemed more plausible.

Finally convinced, Einstein (despite his pacifism) agreed to coauthor a letter with Szilard to Franklin D Roosevelt, urging the American president to start the country's own research into atomic weaponry.

"Certain aspects of the situation seem to call for watchfulness," Einstein wrote in the August 2, 1939, letter. "And, if necessary, quick action on the part of the Administration." If the technology was to be useful after all, they reasoned, it should at least be in the hands of democratic nations.

Although it took some time, and intervention by a sympathetic Alexander Sachs, the letter reached Roosevelt two months later and did in fact move Roosevelt to action. Roosevelt is reported to have indicated his approval for the project to Sachs at the time with the words, "What you are after is to see that the Nazis don't blow us up."

Roosevelt replied to Einstein in a letter dated October 19, 1939. "My dear Professor," he began. "I found this of such import that I have convened a Board [...] to thoroughly investigate the possibilities of your suggestion regarding the element of uranium [...] I feel this is the most practical and effective method of dealing with the subject."

Soon the race between the Allied forces and the Axis powers to develop an atomic bomb was underway.

The New "Ten Commandments"

The magnitude of what was to come, the realization of what the previous decade of scientific advancement now made inevitable, became undeniably real to Szilard. The complexities of the ethical implications of the work that he and Einstein had proposed in the letter to President Roosevelt were clear to him.

Szilard's family was nominally Jewish and observed many of the social rituals of Judaism, but they were not particularly religious. Nonetheless, like many other such secular families, they maintained a connection with the moral values and ethical principles of the religion. Szilard had also deeply studied the philosophy of Rationalism during his time at the university.

Anticipating the difficult decisions ahead, Szilard set out to define a personal moral framework, something he could rely on to address the crises of conscience that he knew were soon to come.

41

In 1940, building on the spiritual foundation of his Judaism and the philosophic foundation of his Rationalism, Szilard penned his own version of the "Ten Commandments":

- Recognize the connections of things and the laws of conduct of men, so that you may know what you are doing.

- Let your acts be directed toward a worthy goal, but do not ask if they will reach it; they are to be models and examples, not means to an end.

- Speak to all men as you do to yourself, with no concern for the effect you make, so that you do not shut them out from your world; lest in isolation the meaning of life slips out of sight and you lose the belief in the perfection of the creation.

- Do not destroy what you cannot create.

- Touch no dish unless you are hungry.

- Do not covet what you cannot have.

- Do not lie without need.

- Honor children. Listen reverently to their words and speak to them with infinite love.

- Do your work for six years; but in the seventh, go into solitude or among strangers, so that the recollection of your friends does not hinder you from being what you have become.

- Lead your life with a gentle hand and be ready to leave whenever you are called.

Szilard didn't share these ethical edicts publicly until 1963, when they were published (only) in the German edition of his book **THE VOICE OF THE DOLPHINS**. According to Trude Szilard, his wife, Leo was never satisfied with attempts to translate his Ten Commandments from German.

Following her husband's death in 1964, Trude sent a letter to a local newspaper, the Coronado Journal, to thank the community for their outpouring of love and support. Included in the letter was an English translation of Szilard's "Ten Commandments," courtesy of Dr. Jacob Bronowski, a friend and colleague from the Salk Institute.

Trude wrote, "To me [the Ten Commandments] represent his true 'Last Will and Testament,' and I want to share it with our friends whose kind words and deeds have given me so much comfort after Leo left me. I got him back a little bit reflected, as it were, in the mirror of his friends." This was the first time that his edicts appeared in print in English.

Trude's letter was published in the September 10 edition of the paper, on page 10, alongside an advertisement for '64 Chevrolets and a photograph from a "Luau"-style farewell party for a local military veteran family.

While the spirit of Szilard's words comes through in their translation to English, there are certain subtleties reflected in the original that are lost between languages.

For example, in the seventh commandment, he writes "Do not lie without need." The German word translated as "need," here, better conveys the meaning as the weight of what is absolutely necessary, almost in an existential sense—what is needed for the greater good, not for one's own good.

In another example, in the tenth point, the "gentle hand" with which one is to lead their life refers less to the metaphorical gentleness of its use than to its lack of burden or baggage.

Then follow the words "be ready to leave whenever you are called," which, to an English reader, may come across in a religious context, as in being called to the heavens; but in the German original, the connotation is of a life's calling, that is, being called to upheave one's life to perform some important duty. Together, these distinctions recall the two suitcases with which Szilard fled the Nazis and which he kept packed, waiting by the door, in every room he slept in for the rest of his life.

The Uranium Club

Szilard's fears about Nazi Germany's plans to develop an atomic bomb were not unfounded. Like the United States, Canada, and England, Germany had embarked on exploratory research into nuclear fission in the late 1930s. But, also like its Allied counterparts, Germany's research into atomic energy wasn't initially considered a high priority for either domestic or military use.

Germany's research program was called the *Uranverein*, or "Uranium Club." The Uranverein's research built on the work of the very physicists and mathematicians who had fled or been expelled by the Nazis: the scientific advancements that the Third Reich had officially dismissed as "Jewish physics."

In June of 1942, physicist Werner Heisenberg, who was a principal scientist in the Uranverein, was asked by Germany's Minister of Armaments about the prospects for applying the organization's work toward developing nuclear weapons. Heisenberg replied that, because of its significant cost and the scarcity of qualified staff, it would take at least three years, and likely longer, to develop such a weapon.

The unspoken truth was that most of the scientists who were well-qualified to work on such a program had already been killed or driven away from Germany.

In an exchange with Bernhard Rust, Hitler's Minister of Education, preeminent German mathematician David Hilbert was asked if Gottingen University, where Hilbert had spent his entire career, had in any way suffered from "the departure of the Jews and their friends." Hilbert replied that the university had not suffered: "it just doesn't exist anymore."

By the time the Nazis realized the strategic potential of a nuclear arms program, the Manhattan Project was already underway in the United States.

To maintain their head start, the Allies established a covert program called the "Alsos Mission," operating under the authority of the Office of Strategic Services (a precursor to today's Central Intelligence Agency). Its charter was to monitor and, if necessary, to sabotage Axis nuclear weapons programs. This was typically accomplished through strategic kidnappings (and occasional assassinations) of German and Italian scientists.

From Committee to Commitment

Whatever the enemy might be planning, American Science will be equal to the challenge.

—President Franklin D. Roosevelt, in a June 29, 1943, letter
to General Leslie Groves

The "Board" that Roosevelt mentioned in his reply to Einstein's letter was called the "Advisory Committee on Uranium." The Committee was founded in 1939 and charged with investigating the possible civilian and military uses of atomic energy.

The committee was chaired by Lyman Briggs, a physicist and engineer who formerly headed the National Bureau of Standards. Although foreign scientists were prohibited from actively serving on the committee, for security reasons, Briggs invited three of the Hungarian Martians (Leo Szilard, Edward Teller, and Eugene Wigner) to its inaugural meeting in Washington, DC, on October 21, 1939. Einstein had declined his own invitation.

Less than two weeks later, the committee approved a $6,000 investment in supplies for Fermi's lab at Columbia University, including the uranium and graphite that he and Szilard needed for their preliminary experiments with building a nuclear reactor. The committee also submitted a letter to President Roosevelt, stating that while the theory of nuclear chain reactions had not yet been verified in the lab, the magnitude of its potential wartime applications warranted additional investment.

Within a year, the Advisory Committee on Uranium was superseded, in June of 1940, by the newly established National Defense Research Committee (NDRC). The NDRC was responsible for several critical research projects, including the development of radar, amphibious vehicles, atomic energy, and, under a research project run by behavioral psychologist BF Skinner, the possibility of using pigeons to guide bombs. Critically, the NDRC also enforced a ban on the publication of any research related to developments into uranium, nuclear fission, and any other topic related to nuclear science.

Responsibility for overseeing the research into atomic weaponry was soon shifted to another body. In June of 1941, Roosevelt signed an executive order establishing the Office of Scientific Research and Development (OSRD), which was granted the authority, resources, and a $300,000 budget to continue the work of the NDRC.

Roosevelt appointed Vannevar Bush as Director of the OSRD. Bush had been involved in oversight of the uranium program from its inception and was well-regarded as an effective administrator with a strong background in science and engineering.

Bush organized a complex network of government agencies, academic institutions, and private corporations to engage in different aspects of the research aimed at realizing the potential use of uranium. This collaboration involved the University of Chicago, Princeton University, Columbia University, and the University of Virginia, as well as companies like Westinghouse, H. Kellogg, Standard Oil, and Union Carbide. He also made informal connections with organizations in the United Kingdom and Canada that were working on related research.

In his preliminary report to Roosevelt, Bush expressed confidence in the program and estimated that a prototype nuclear reactor was likely to be constructed by the following summer, at which point he recommended turning the project, referred to by the administration simply as "Section S-1," over to the War Department.

The United States officially entered World War II in December of 1941, following the Japanese attack on Pearl Harbor. A few months into 1942, after almost a year's work on the project, Bush reported back to the President on the program's progress, including sharing the results of critical research conducted by Robert Oppenheimer on the uranium-235 isotope. As Bush had recommended, Roosevelt moved responsibility for the program under the auspices of the Army Corps of Engineers.

The Manhattan Engineer District

I was horrified. It seemed as if the whole endeavor was founded on possibilities rather than probabilities. Of theory there was a great deal, of proven knowledge not much. Even if the theories were correct, the engineering difficulties would be unprecedented.

—Leslie Groves, from his autobiography **Now It Can Be Told: The Story of the Manhattan Project**

I was not interested in, and did not read about, economics or politics [...] I was deeply interested in my science; but I had no understanding of the relations of man to his society.

—J Robert Oppenheimer, 1954

Brigadier General Leslie Groves was appointed by Roosevelt to command the military program. The Army Corps of Engineers convention at the time was to name research projects after the location of their headquarters, which in this case was an office building on Broadway, a few blocks from New York's City Hall. Groves famously shortened "Manhattan Engineer District" to "Manhattan Project," a name which stuck.

Groves had a reputation for getting things done and had just completed oversight of the construction of the Pentagon. By comparison, his new project had a small budget: the construction of the Pentagon cost approximately $83 million dollars, and the Manhattan Project had an initial budget that was only a little more than half that sum.

While Groves oversaw the administration of the Manhattan Project, responsibility for the scientific operations was given to J Robert Oppenheimer, who had been officially involved in nuclear research for the United States for some time. There were serious concerns about his political affiliations with the Communist Party, but Groves felt so strongly about the appointment that he personally overrode the security requirements for Oppenheimer.

Oppenheimer insisted that, to foster deeper and more efficient collaboration, key scientists on the project should be based in a central laboratory. Oppenheimer's family had been leasing property in the Sangre de Cristo Mountains in New Mexico and suggested a nearby site as a suitable location for the proposed lab. It was suitably distant from either coast, and suitably remote, so his proposal was approved.

The government exercised its legal right to eminent domain, taking possession of a suitably large and remote parcel of land in New Mexico that had been home to a school for ranchers. This became "Project Y," in the hastily constructed "closed city" of Los Alamos, the top secret site for principal research into the atomic bomb.

Make Trouble, Not Bombs

From a scientific perspective, Leo Szilard was an obvious fit for work on the Manhattan Project. But a report by Army Intelligence into the physicist's political leanings raised serious concerns. Szilard, despite having fled Hitler's Germany, was described as "pro-German," and it was noted that he had professed a belief that the Germans would win the war. The report concluded with a warning that Szilard was unsuitable for employment on "matters of a secret nature."

A concurrent FBI investigation disagreed on the assessment of Szilard's suitability for the project. The report quoted Einstein, who described Szilard as "reliable, trustworthy, honest, and gifted." Most importantly, despite having fought on the side of the Germans in World War I, Szilard was confirmed by the FBI as solidly anti-Nazi.

Neither the Army Intelligence nor FBI reports commented on Szilard's awkward, contrarian, and aggressive communication style nor his impatience with authority of any kind.

General Groves developed an intense dislike and distrust of Szilard over the duration of the project. He authorized secret surveillance of the physicist throughout the war and even considered placing him under military custody until the end of the project.

The Manhattan Project employed over 100,000 workers between 1942 and 1945. Of these, an estimated 1,000 were aware that the work they were engaged in related to atomic science. And perhaps a few dozen people employed by the Manhattan Project had a complete picture of what was being built. The others, quoting a LIFE magazine article from just after the war, "worked like moles in the dark."

Szilard, of course, was one of these few dozen who knew what was being built, and appreciated its gravity. With his conscience buttressed by his freshly penned Ten Commandments, he proved to be a constant cause of frustration to his superiors on the project.

Szilard, now based at the University of Chicago's Met Lab, disregarded security rules that he considered unnecessary or that should not apply to him. He called for open conversation and debate among the scientists involved in the project and constantly raised ethical concerns over what was being built. When confronted about his apparent disregard for the "compartmentalization" of various aspects of the project, he insisted that if the technology was being developed within a democratic country, a democratic approach to the science was warranted as well.

Szilard was especially concerned about what plans the United States had for the atomic bomb, if it were successfully built: would it be used as a deterrent, as he and many of his fellow scientists hoped, or would it actually be deployed, as he and many of his fellow scientists feared? If Roosevelt's administration had specific plans in this regard, those engaged in the research and development were given no indication.

On July 16, 1945, the Manhattan Project culminated in the first successful detonation of an atomic bomb, the so-called "Gadget," at the Trinity test site in Alamogordo, New Mexico. Roosevelt had died three months earlier, on April 12, about a month before the German surrender.

The decision about what to do with the atomic bomb now fell to his successor, Harry S Truman. The answer came in the form of over 200,000 civilian deaths in the Japanese cities of Hiroshima and Nagasaki on August 6 and 9 of 1945. It was the devastation of these cities, not Wells's Berlin, that brought about the end of the war.

Reflection

Szilard took Wells's warnings to heart. When he saw that it would be impossible to forestall the development of atomic weaponry, he dedicated himself to mitigating the threat that the new technology posed to the world.

In the next chapter, we'll see how Szilard's moral and ethical resolve inspired many of his peers to exercise their consciences and help organize against this threat.

CHAPTER 3

The World Set Free?

Once the atomic bomb became a reality, there was intense debate between the scientists who had been involved in the weapons program and the politicians who oversaw it about if, and how, it should be used.

The final decision fell to Harry S Truman, who had ascended to the presidency after the death of Roosevelt in April of 1945. Truman, who had served as Roosevelt's vice president, was probably unaware of the Manhattan Project until he took the presidency. The decision he faced now would change the course of history.

The Decision to Drop the Bombs

The target will be a purely military one and we will issue a warning statement asking the [Japanese] to surrender and save lives. I'm sure they will not do that, but we will have given them the chance.

> —Harry S Truman, in a diary entry from July 25, 1945

When you have to deal with a beast, you have to treat him as a beast.

> —Harry S Truman, explaining his decision to bomb Hiroshima and Nagasaki without warning, in a letter to the Federal Council of Churches

© Coraline Ada Ehmke 2025
C. A. Ehmke, *We Just Build Hammers*, https://doi.org/10.1007/979-8-8688-1249-1_3

Truman's predecessor had earned a reputation for strategically keeping information close to his chest, sharing just enough to keep his administration going but holding on to anything that might prove of value to himself or to his opponents. As such, he left no record or other indication of his intentions regarding the use of the atomic bomb. Truman was on his own and had to turn to his advisors for recommendations.

In a June 21, 1945 report, Truman's so-called Interim Committee, after some deliberation, recommended the immediate use of the bomb against Japan, emphasizing that it be used without any sort of advance warning. The committee stressed that two targets should be selected, based not only on their strategic military value but also on their proximity to "homes or other buildings most susceptible to damage."

Their recommendation also called for the unilateral revocation of Clause Two of the Quebec Agreement: a treaty between the United States, United Kingdom, and Canada guaranteeing that the atomic bomb would not be used without consulting or at least informing the other two nations. The two-and-a-half page report was signed by R Gordon Arneson, an Army lieutenant and Interim Committee secretary.

A memo titled "Recommendations on the Immediate Use of Nuclear Weapons," penned by Manhattan Project chief scientist J Robert Oppenheimer and cosigned by Enrico Fermi, came to the same conclusion. Oppenheimer wrote that "we can propose no technical demonstration likely to bring an end to the war; we see no alternative to direct military use."

Dissenting Voices

The opinions of our scientific colleagues on the initial use of these weapons are not unanimous.

—J Robert Oppenheimer, "Recommendations on the
Immediate Use of Nuclear Weapons," June 16, 1945

Others in the administration and military came to different conclusions about the immediate use of the bomb. The alternative that had the most support was the idea of some sort of demonstration of the bomb's capabilities that would impress the Japanese enough to bring about their unconditional surrender. It was noted that the devastation of the atomic bomb would provide an opportunity for the country to "save face" rather than admitting defeat through conventional warfare. This option was promoted by officials including Truman's Secretary of War and the Undersecretary of the Navy.

Oppenheimer, Fermi, and a minority of others notwithstanding, there was also significant support for a nonlethal demonstration of the bomb among those scientists who had been involved in its development.

Farrington Daniels, director of the Metallurgical Laboratory in Chicago (which had focused on plutonium research and was the site of the first nuclear reactor), even conducted a poll of section chiefs and their groups: only 23 out of 150 polled (15%) advocated for immediate use of the bomb in the way that was determined most prompt by the military; 69 (46%) for a military demonstration in Japan, followed by opportunity to surrender; 39 (26%) for a demonstration in the United States with Japanese representatives present; 16 (11%) called for a public demonstration without subsequent use by the military; and 3 (2%) called for the bomb to not be used in any way and for the technology to be kept secret.

The Franck Report

We found ourselves, by the force of events, the last five years in the position of a small group of citizens cognizant of a grave danger for the safety of this country as well as for the future of all the other nations, of which the rest of mankind is unaware.

—Franck Report, June 1945

The Committee on Political and Social Problems of the Metallurgical Laboratory, representing a group of atomic scientists and chaired by physicist James Franck, submitted its own recommendations to the administration.

While acknowledging the inevitability of the knowledge of atomic weaponry becoming widely known, this alternative committee called for the technology to be shared with US allies and placed under international control. It recommended a public demonstration of the country's nuclear capabilities in an uninhabited location with members of the newly chartered United Nations as witnesses.

The Franck Report, as it has come to be known, concluded by urging that "the use of nuclear bombs in this war be considered as a problem of long-range national policy rather than military expediency." Its authors insisted that the United States carry out a policy that would be "directed primarily to the achievement of an agreement permitting an effective international control of the means of nuclear warfare."

The Szilard Petition

Not surprisingly, Leo Szilard also held very strong convictions about how the bomb should be used—or, rather, not used. In July of 1945, he circulated a petition to 70 scientists who were engaged in various aspects of the Manhattan Project at the Oak Ridge facility in Tennessee and the Metallurgical Laboratory in Chicago. The petition called for a demonstration of the atomic bomb, rather than its immediate military use, to force Japan to surrender.

In Szilard's cover letter accompanying the petition, addressed to its scientific audience, he acknowledged that there was only a small chance that the petition might influence the course of events. However, he still saw value in recording the opposition, on moral grounds, of a large number of scientists, ensuring that it was part of the historical record.

While the Franck Report emphasized the role of international cooperation to contain the threat of the new atomic bomb, Szilard's petition bore a more impassioned tone. Its signatories agreed that if the United States were to deploy the bomb solely based on immediate military advantage, the country would "bear the responsibility of opening the door to an era of devastation on an unimaginable scale," thereby losing its moral authority among the other nations of the world.

"The added material strength which this lead gives to the United States brings with it the obligation of restraint," Szilard wrote, "and if we were to violate this obligation our moral position would be weakened in the eyes of the world and in our own eyes." Ignoring what he called the ethical "obligation of restraint" could unleash unimaginable forces of destruction upon the world and spark an arms race that would be difficult, if not impossible, to keep under control.

The petition never made it through the chain of command to President Truman and was not even made public until 1961.

A Race to Arms

Many of the scientists who have been working on S-1 have expressed considerable concern about the future dangers of the development of atomic power. Some are fearful that no safe system of international control can be established. They, therefore, envisage the possibility of an armament race that may threaten civilization.

—George Harrison, "Memorandum for the Secretary of War," June 26, 1945

It was clear to Szilard and his peers that the consequences of the atomic bomb would haunt humanity for the foreseeable future. It was not difficult for him to see that the chain reaction set in motion with the devastating conclusion of World War II would only intensify the strained relations between the United States and the Soviet Union.

55

A small group of atomic scientists sought to circumvent the increasingly hostile relations between the two nations by arranging meetings between Soviet and American scientists. Their hope was that, in building relationships outside of the influence of politicians, they could find common ground in each other's rationality and come together to avoid a nuclear arms race and its threat of global destruction: what came to be called the Cold War.

But once World War II ended, Szilard and many others who once had the ear of President Roosevelt had no vestige of influence with his successor, President Truman. The decades-long struggle for nuclear supremacy that so many had feared now seemed inevitable.

The atomic scientists would have to find other ways to avert further catastrophes arising from their work.

An Open Conspiracy

I do not believe that permanent peace can be had at any lesser cost than the cost of a World Government.

—Leo Szilard

I am discussing whether our species is to live or die.

—H.G. Wells

Szilard's time in Berlin had given him the scientific foundation that shaped his contributions to atomic science. His rationalist philosophy, socialist ideology, and antifascist politics shaped how he dealt with the aftermath of these contributions. And if these failed him, he could always turn to Wells.

For years after reading **THE WORLD SET FREE** in 1923, Szilard remained an avid fan of the writing of H.G. Wells. The two had even met over dinner in 1929, at the house of a mutual friend, Otto Mandl. Szilard was a friend of Mandl's daughter, Gerda, and called on the family often that summer. Mandl, as it turned out, was responsible for Wells's work being published in German.

Szilard engaged in a lively conversation with Wells over the writer's most recent book, titled **An Open Conspiracy**, which was published the previous year. Szilard found Wells's political ideas well-aligned with his own. The two ended the evening in agreement that the current state of governments and institutions around the world left humanity ill-equipped to deal with the inevitable crises ahead.

Wells's book proposed that, in order to save humanity from its "dangers, uncertainties and miseries," a group of individuals must be gathered together, representing in their number all classes and kinds from all communities in all nations. This group, this "conspiracy" of individuals, was called upon to steer the world to a more just future. Their work would transition the governance of the world from violent, provisional national governments to global institutions providing for the health, well-being, and fundamental rights of all the people of the world.

Now, at the end of World War II, Szilard drew on his memory of Wells's proposal. Wells had envisioned a future governed by science and rationality. But scientists had failed to bring rationality to the sphere of politics; it was now upon them to create their own "open conspiracy." Without being able to rely on politicians, Szilard and his scientific coconspirators would have to find some way to save the world themselves.

Bulletin of the Atomic Scientist

Scientists at the "Met Lab" (Metallurgical Laboratory), the Chicago site of Manhattan Project research, had lobbied hard for the nonlethal use of the atomic bomb. Once the bomb was used against Japan and World War II came to its conclusion, these scientists immediately undertook projects to try to contain the technology that they had helped unleash.

One such project was the **BULLETIN OF THE ATOMIC SCIENTIST**. Created by a group of scientists including Szilard, Einstein, and biophysicist Eugene Rabinowitch, it was initially circulated as a mimeographed newsletter to other scientists at the Met Lab.

In 1947, the group decided that the **BULLETIN** could be more widely circulated, outside the Met Lab, as a monthly magazine. Their intent was to encourage discussion and collaboration among scientists worldwide, across political borders. This was a position that Szilard had long advocated for and, in fact, had nearly been imprisoned for during his Manhattan Project days.

The cover of the first magazine edition of the **BULLETIN** was designed by a Chicago-based artist named Martyl Langsdorf. Her husband, Alexander Langsdorf, had worked on the Manhattan Project with **BULLETIN** coeditor Hyman Goldsmith. As a publication with almost no money, the cover would have to consist of a simple design. There wasn't much room for an illustration, and the budget permitted only two colors for printing. But Langsdorf found a solution and created what may be the single most powerful work of information design ever created: the Doomsday Clock.

Langsdorf considered many options before arriving at the idea of a simple clock face to represent the impending danger inherent to the Atomic Age. Recognizing the increasing post-War tension between the United States and the Soviet Union, she wanted a symbol that would communicate the urgency and precarity of the arms race, hoping to "frighten the world into rationality."

So she sketched a clock, using the back cover of a book of Beethoven's "Piano Sonatas" as a canvas. The clock was intended to suggest that time to get this new technology under control was short.

The Doomsday Clock, as it was dubbed, was initially drawn with its hands reading seven minutes to midnight. Since its conception in 1947, every subsequent issue of the **BULLETIN OF THE ATOMIC SCIENTIST** has featured the clock on its cover. And the time on the clock is always adjusted this way or that in response to the changing world political situation.

Council for a Livable World

*We may take the stand that those who have originated this ter-
rible weapon and those who have materially contributed to its
development, have, before God and the World, the duty to see
to it that it should be ready to be used only at the proper time
and in the proper way.*

—Leo Szilard

Another institution that Leo Szilard helped to bring into the world is
the Council for a Livable World. It was founded in 1962 under the name
"Council for Abolishing War." The Council is considered to be a first-of-its-
kind operation, organized as a political action committee.

The Council oversees a research operation called the Center for Arms
Control and Non-Proliferation, which for decades has served members
and staff of the US Congress with research and policy recommendations.
The Center operates as a nonprofit, nonpartisan organization dedicated to
"reducing and eliminating the threats" of nuclear, chemical, and biological
weapons.

The organization also endorses congressional candidates who support
arms control and other non-proliferation-related national and global
security policies.

Its influence remains strong, with accomplishments over the past
several decades including chemical warfare research ban treaties,
preventing funding for so-called "bunker buster" bombs, blocking
President Clinton's "National Missile Defense" initiative, and discouraging
other similar advancements in weapons of mass destruction.

"My Trial As a War Prisoner"

"If they cannot take it straight, they will get it in fiction."

—Leo Szilard, quoted in *Toward a Livable World*

Speculative fiction, and in particular the works of H.G. Wells, played a huge role in shaping Leo Szilard's scientific contributions, as well as his philosophical and ethical outlooks regarding the technologies that he helped create. Interestingly, Szilard even tried his own hand at fiction, perhaps as a way of exploring his complex feelings of necessity and guilt, hope and hopelessness.

In 1947, Szilard wrote himself into a short satirical piece he titled "My Trial as a War Criminal." Through the work, he considered the responsibility that he and his fellow atomic scientists bore for the impact of their work.

In the story, Szilard himself is held to account for his alleged war crimes related to inducing the United States to develop an atomic bomb and its subsequent use against Japan in World War II. The story takes place after World War III, which the Russians have won by means of biological warfare.

His prosecutors question why he had not engaged in the peaceful application of atomic energy in the years between the wars. Szilard replies that he had "five good and valid reasons" (none of which are specified in the story itself) that were dutifully noted by his interrogators in shorthand.

His trial takes place in Lake Success, a town in Long Island in New York which served as the temporary home for the United Nations from 1946 to 1951. The judge in the case determined that, as there was no precedent for destroying cities with atomic bombs, the bombings had been a "violation of the customs of war," and thus qualified as a war crime. It didn't matter if the bombings were intended to bring World War II to a conclusion before even more lives were lost to conventional warfare.

In a dizzying *deus ex machina*, Szilard's fate is decided when the entirety of the Russian population is suddenly wiped out by the accidental release of its own biological weapons from their storage facilities.

At the time of its writing, Szilard was strongly discouraged from publishing the story, especially with the raw political emotions remaining immediately following World War II. The fear was that nationalistic tensions would have made the average reader suspicious of or even hostile toward Szilard's treatment of the subject of the uncertainty of humanity's post-War survival.

When it was finally published, nearly two decades later, "My Trial as a War Criminal" became required reading in universities throughout the world, including Harvard Law School. According to Szilard biographer William Lanouette, the story even provided inspiration to Soviet physicist and human rights activist Andrei Sakharov, famous for his opposition to the USSR's role in the nuclear arms race in the decades following World War II.

The Voice of the Dolphins

Where the spirit of science is surely understood, you will know that as a matter of fact prophecy has always been inseparably associated with the idea of scientific research.

—H.G. Wells, in an address to the Royal Institution
of London

"My Trial as a War Criminal" was eventually published in Szilard's 1961 book of short stories, **THE VOICE OF THE DOLPHINS**. Most of the other stories in the book had also been written in the 1940s. The titular story, however, was dictated into a tape recorder in 1960 from Szilard's hospital bed.

By imitating the style and affect of speculative fiction writers like Wells and others, in particular through the mechanic of a future history, Szilard was able to reach beyond scientific and political circles and appeal to a broader audience. Today, the book is considered a classic of the speculative fiction genre.

The English version of the book comprised five stories authored by Szilard, but it began with a 1938 poem by Stephen Vincent Benét titled "Nightmare for Future Reference." The poem, telling a story of endless war, sets the mood for the rest of the book, albeit without the jarring humor that Szilard sometimes peppered his own stories with.

The poem concludes with the sudden drop-off of humanity's birth rate and chillingly declares:

> *And we keep the toys in the stores, and the colored books, And people marry and plan and the rest of it, But, you see, there aren't any children. They aren't born.*

Szilard considered the book his "political testament." The themes of the stories revolve around the facts and fictions of the Cold War and are particularly critical of the selfish irrationality and immorality of governmental and scientific institutions. (It is worth remembering, however, that his "Ten Commandments," his most direct writing on ethics and morality, was only published in the German edition of the book.)

Following the poem by Benét is the longest story in the book, "The Voice of the Dolphins." The antipolitical slogan repeated among politicians in the story, that "scientists should be on tap, not on top," certainly reflects Szilard's frustration at how little say the Manhattan Project scientists had over how their work was used. In the story, the scientific community manages to sidestep political barriers and establish a facility in Vienna nominally for the study of molecular biology. But, in a nod to John Lilly's 1960 assertion that dolphins might have their own language, might be able to mimic human speech, and may have equal or superior intelligence to humans, Szilard had the scientists at the Vienna Institute instead set out to solve the problems of humanity through consultation with a pod of extraordinary dolphins.

The next story, titled "The Mark Gable Foundation," was written in 1948. Reminiscent of Wells's **THE TIME MACHINE**, the unnamed narrator, who wanted to see what the world would be like in 300 years, arranges to be frozen, or "withdrawn from life" as the process is called, until the year 2260. However, he is awakened after only 90 years and learns the facts of a strange new way of life on earth. Teeth had become unfashionable, and the richest man on earth, Mark Gable, had made his fortune by selling his sperm and producing millions of "donated children," each of which earned him thousands of dollars in royalties.

His 1949 "Calling All Stars" consists of a broadcast sent throughout the universe by a civilization of 100 disembodied minds from the planet Cybernetica. The message is an urgent call to any sentient being who may receive it. One of the minds, Mind 59, deduces the existence and evolution of organic life as a way of explaining the observation of uranium explosions on the surface of the distant planet Earth. "If there exist organisms on Earth which are not subject to the laws of reason, our society is in danger," the message warns. The story ends with a desperate call for help from any other unknown minds in the galaxy who have knowledge of Earth: "Please respond. Please respond."

Finally, the whimsical and pseudo-archeological "Report on 'Grand Central Terminal'" closes out the book. The story posits travelers from space who arrive on earth just to find that during the decade of their travel, all life on the planet has already become extinct. Just like the jarred brains of Cybernetica, the travelers had observed mysterious flashes of light across the planet. Upon their arrival, they detected radioactivity of a sort that could not be explained by natural processes. But, "since the earth-dwellers who built all these cities must have been rational beings," the visitors presume that humans wouldn't have invested in all the trouble of harnessing the atom "just in order to destroy themselves."

Szilard lived to see the world's reaction to his book before his death in 1964, but did not live long enough to see some of its prophecies about the Cold War come true.

He was remembered by his wife and his grandnieces and grandnephews with an epitaph he wrote himself: "He Did His Best."

Reflection

We've seen how Leo Szilard and his fellow scientists responded to the devastating technology they had unleashed on the world, with their efforts spawning projects like the Doomsday Clock and the Bulletin of the Atomic Scientist.

But atomic bombs were not the only legacy of World War II nor the only legacy of Leo Szilard. Long before the war, and before the real start of his career, his dissertation proposed a novel solution to the Maxwell's Demon paradox: representing information as a quantum phenomenon.

Almost by accident, Szilard's idea helped usher in the field of information theory. This opened the way to the development of the computing machine and the next great Industrial Revolution, with its own set of ethical dilemmas.

PART II

The Parable of the Locksmith

CHAPTER 4

The Parable of the Locksmith

As nuclear scientists scrambled to contain the technology behind the splitting of the atom, another group of scientists was just beginning to come into its own.

Out of necessity, World War II brought heavy investment in analog and digital computing machines. The Nazis had made tremendous advances since World War I in encrypted communication. The Allied forces responded by allocating significant time and energy to codebreaking efforts, necessitating the rapid evolution of computing machinery to crack the Nazi codes.

Computers would soon have as much impact on the world as the harnessing of the atom, but as we will learn, they also brought their own set of unique ethical challenges.

The Third Industrial Revolution

Thus the new industrial revolution is a two-edged sword. It may be used for the benefit of humanity, but only if humanity survives long enough to enter a period in which such a benefit is possible. It may also be used to destroy humanity, and if it is not used intelligently it can go very far in that direction.

—Norbert Wiener, *The Human Use of Human Beings*, 1954

© Coraline Ada Ehmke 2025
C. A. Ehmke, *We Just Build Hammers*, https://doi.org/10.1007/979-8-8688-1249-1_4

The Third Industrial Revolution, sometimes referred to as the Digital Revolution, followed fast on the end of World War II, with governments, academic researchers, and private corporations imagining new uses for another groundbreaking wartime technology, one that brought unprecedented computational power and speed into the world.

Throughout history, technological progress has often been dictated by the needs and priorities of governments and especially their militaries. The birth of the Digital Revolution was no different: the major powers in the world invested heavily in computing to meet their immediate needs during World War II but continued to pour money into the nascent field as the inevitability of the Cold War became clearer.

The earliest (nonhuman) computers were complex electromechanical machines. Each computer was designed and constructed to solve a particular kind of problem using a predefined, fixed, and permanent instruction set. Changing this instruction set involved physically modifying the computer's circuitry and mechanical elements.

Reprogramming a single-function computer was a labor-intensive and expensive prospect. It required a team of operators, usually women, to design the new program, a crew of engineers to rebuild the circuitry, and weeks of testing before a new program could be executed.

This is the level of computing technology with which both the Axis and the Allied powers went into World War II.

Stored-Program Computers

As early as 1936, however, computer scientists began exploring alternatives to the fixed-program computer architecture. In a seminal paper titled "On Computable Numbers," English mathematician Alan Turing, who would soon lead the Allies' codebreaking effort in World War II, proposed a new kind of computer altogether. Turing envisioned a computer designed to be easily reprogrammed, a flexible device whose fundamental functions could be defined on the fly.

Similar ideas were percolating in other parts of the world. In Germany, a scientist named Konrad Zuse filed patents in 1936 and 1937 that anticipated stored-program computing. The first, submitted in May 1936, described a "Mechanisches Schaltglied," a mechanical switching element that was a predecessor to tube switches (or "valves"). The second patent, filed the following July, revealed the intended use of these mechanical switches. "Aus mechanischen Schaltgliedern aufgebautes Speicherwerk," which translates to "A storage mechanism made up of mechanical switching elements," outlined a scheme for combining these mechanical switches to create a mechanism for storing data in a kind of physical memory construction.

A Faustian Bargain

As in Faust, we find Mephistophelian figures in the company of many inventors and discoverers. Only too often the inventor is the idealist who tries to improve the world, only to be crushed by harsh realities ... he is forced to do business with the wielders of power.

—Konrad Zuse

In 1938, Konrad Zuse became the first computer scientist to realize the dream of a programmable computer. He constructed a prototype, the Z1, out of spare parts in the living room of his Berlin flat. While the Z1 suffered from mechanical problems, the machine proved that a general-purpose arithmetical computing machine was possible. The computer was capable of solving any problem that could be answered with a "true" or "false" response—essentially, Boolean logic—and on any value that could be represented in binary.

Although it was not proven at the time, the Z1 is today understood to have been Turing-complete; that is, it fit the constraints defined by Alan Turing for a machine capable of being programmed to solve any basic type of problem that could be expressed in code.

Zuse continued iterating on the architecture of the computer in his apartment. In 1941, he arranged to demonstrate the functionality of his new Z3 prototype to the German government. The Nazis immediately saw the potential of the machines and began funding his work in earnest.

Eventually, this work led to a series of successors to the Z1 and Z3, which were employed to conduct aerodynamic calculations for radio-controlled flying bombs, the early precursors to modern cruise missiles. Many of the machines that Zuse built for the Nazis were destroyed during Allied bombing campaigns, but the work continued.

Zuse is not known to have expressed any doubts or regrets about his contributions to the Nazi war effort. After the end of the war, when challenged on this point, he simply shrugged the question off and opined that the best scientists and engineers often have to make "Faustian bargains" in order to continue their work.

IBM, whose Germany subsidiary had supplied census computing devices to the Nazi government, snatched up Zuse's patents immediately after the war. For the rest of the world, Zuse's innovations were not recognized outside of Germany until decades later.

The Heath Robinson

Meanwhile, at the Government Code and Cypher School in Bletchley Park, about 50 miles northwest of London, Alan Turing was using computers to perform cryptanalysis of Nazi communications. To assist in the codebreaking effort, Turing and a team of engineers and scientists built a machine they called the "Heath Robinson." This was a reference to a British cartoonist who, like the American Rube Goldberg, was known for drawing comically complex machines.

The Heath Robinson was not a general-purpose computer like the Z1 and its descendants, but rather was custom-designed for a single purpose: decoding encrypted text. It was able to read data from paper tape at a rate of over 2,000 characters per second, a remarkable achievement for the time, and absolutely necessary for handling the vast amounts of data required for decoding.

While the Heath Robinson and its descendants plugged away at the problem of deciphering the Lorenz and Enigma ciphers, new experimental computers were also being installed at Bletchley. These included the fixed-function Colossus, developed by English engineer Tommy Flowers.

Colossus

Like the Z1, Colossus operated on binary-encoded data, but instead of using mechanical switches and relays, it relied on nearly 2,000 "valves" or vacuum tubes. Colossus was more than twice as fast as the Heath Robinson, with a read rate of 5,000 characters per second, and was able to store 501 binary bits on hundreds of switches and across a series of hot-pluggable panels.

The Colossus famously decoded communications confirming that Hitler had no plans to move additional troops to bolster Nazi defenses at Normandy, which led then-Commanding General Dwight Eisenhower to green-light plans for the Normandy beach landing. By the end of the war, there were a dozen Colossus computers operating around the clock at Bletchley.

After the war, British Prime Minister Winston Churchill ordered all of the Colossus computers dismantled and destroyed, specifying that the machines were to be reduced to pieces no larger than a fist. Churchill likely made this decision to keep England's codebreaking capabilities a secret post-war.

The Harvard Mark 1

Meanwhile, in Los Alamos, Leo Szilard's colleague and fellow Hungarian Martian John von Neumann was circulating Turing's 1936 paper to the other scientists working at the lab. The dominant computing technology at the start of the Manhattan Project consisted of punch card–operated computing machines from IBM, but before the end of the war, von Neumann also had access to the Harvard Mark 1, cementing his long-term interest in computing and leading to a number of future innovations.

The Mark 1 was a US-built electromechanical computer, created at the Harvard Computation Laboratory by computer science pioneers Grace Hopper and Edmund Berkeley, working under Howard Aiken.

In 1944, von Neumann used the computer to perform vital calculations related to the detonation of the atomic bomb. Unlike the Colossus, which was built for rapid processing operations, the Mark 1's calculating speed was actually slower than the IBM punch card computers. But, critically, the Mark 1 was able to compute values up to 18 decimal places, triple the accuracy of its predecessors.

Cold-War Computing

By the end of the war, the state of the art in computing machinery had made large strides, and the potential for faster calculations, more flexible programming capabilities, and increased data storage seemed to be just over the horizon.

Most of the funding for future advancements consisted of a line item on military budgets. In 1946, the US military invited top thinkers among computer scientists, engineers, and mathematicians from around the world to attend a course series at the University of Pennsylvania. The Moore School of Electrical Engineering at the University was the birthplace of the ENIAC computer, developed for the US Army's ballistics program.

The course series was titled "Theory and Techniques for Design of Digital Computers" and consisted of eight weeks of lectures, five days a week. The lectures were given not only by Moore School staff but by researchers from academia, the military, and a handful of private corporations. Prominent lecturers included John von Neumann and Howard Aiken, both of whom had been actively involved in developing computing technology since World War II, as well as a number of prominent mathematicians and other experts in the field.

Military Computing

The Moore School Lectures, which lasted nearly the entire summer of 1946, sparked continued interest in advancing the field of computing. The series inspired a number of projects throughout government, academic, and corporate circles, but much of the work to advance the field still came through military funding and with military oversight.

The military applications of computing seemed obvious, and the impact of computers on both sides of the war was irrefutable. From the codebreaking computers of Bletchley Park, to the computation machines at Los Alamos, to the programmable computers used by the Nazis to design their V1 missiles, it was clear that computers were now a permanent part of global military operations.

Many of the scientists who had participated in wartime efforts to advance computing technology continued to work for the military afterward. These included Harvard Mark I veteran Grace Hopper, who helped develop the UNIVAC I computer, the COBOL programming language, and the world's first code compiler. Mathematician Norbert Wiener, who founded the field of "cybernetics," helped develop control systems for antiaircraft weapons. Pres Eckert and John Mauchly, the developers of ENIAC, founded the first private computer company and worked almost exclusively with the US military.

Civilian Computing

Computers soon took their place as essential tools for scientists and researchers working in a wide range of fields, including physics, chemistry, and biology. There were also applications in economics, meteorology, sociology, and other fields that required analysis of large quantitative datasets.

Corporations were beginning to bring in computers for business operations, including inventory, accounting, and payroll functions. Still, after the war, many of the scientists and engineers who had been engaged in military research and development found it difficult to secure jobs, let alone funding for their own ventures, with half of their resumes redacted for national security reasons.

Alan Turing, for example, was unable to talk about his work at Bletchley Park, owing to the Official Secrets Act, and thus unable to convince investors that his ideas for the future of computing were even feasible. He was forced to return to his job at Cambridge and continued working on revolutionary designs for computers that he would not see built during his lifetime.

Tommy Flowers, the architect of the Colossus, faced similar obstacles, failing to raise funds for his own computing company. He had only been paid £1,000 for his work on Colossus, most of which he had distributed to his team. He was unable to secure a bank loan to start a computer business, because the banks he petitioned didn't consider the computer he described to be feasible. He returned to work for the British Postal Office working on telephone technology, and his work on computing remained relatively unknown until the 1970s.

Edmund Berkeley, who had worked (with his colleague Grace Hopper) on the Harvard Mark 1 under Howard Aiken, returned to his job at insurance giant Prudential, until his anti-nuclear-weapon activism forced him out of a job. He went into private consulting and in 1947 cofounded the Association for Computing Machinery, the first and largest nonprofit organization for computer scientists, boasting over a hundred-thousand members today.

Berkeley also started a monthly magazine, **Computers AND AUTOMATION**, in 1951. The first regularly published computer magazine, **COMPUTERS AND AUTOMATION**, published an inventory or census of organizations that used computers in their operations, as well as reviews of the latest computing devices from the likes of IBM.

Introducing Neil Macdonald

Little is known about the life of Neil Macdonald, outside of his role as associate editor of **COMPUTERS AND AUTOMATION**. His close association with Edmund Berkeley suggests that he had experience in computer science dating back to the war years. His 1988 obituary, published in the **ANNALS OF THE HISTORY OF COMPUTING**, characterizes Macdonald as a prolific albeit not widely known writer, and most of what is known about Macdonald's character has to be gleaned from a close reading of his contributions to Berkeley's magazine, consisting mainly of playful puzzles and profound thought experiments for his readers.

Macdonald's name is not usually heard in the company of Howard Aiken, Alan Turing, and John von Neumann, but his contribution to the field of computing was profound, as he asked questions that few other computer scientists felt compelled (or safe enough) to ask.

Ballot on Discussion of Social Responsibility

Re your note in the January issue of 'Computers and Automation'—Let's not be quiet! By all means, raise hell! A little more noise is needed at this point in our history.

—Robert Tscudin, from a letter to the editor published in
COMPUTERS AND AUTOMATION, April 1958

Macdonald's political views started becoming apparent several years into his tenure on the magazine.

In the "Readers and Editors Forum" section of the April 1958 edition of **COMPUTERS AND AUTOMATION**, Macdonald described the results of a survey sent out to the magazine's 18,000 subscribers as well as other "computer people."

The survey was sent as an addendum to a letter requesting up-to-date biographical information for a "Who's Who" of computing. The envelope also included a ballot for voting on whether the magazine should publish discussions about the social responsibility of computer scientists. (Respondents to the letter were promised a free copy of **A PICTORIAL MANUAL ON COMPUTERS**, published in digest form the previous year.)

"In **COMPUTERS AND AUTOMATION** we have been discussing recently the social responsibility of computer scientists," the ballot began, "and the relation of computers and automatic guidance systems to ballistic missiles and war." Then, the question was posed, "Do you think we should discuss and argue the social responsibility of computer scientists? Or do you think that we should stick to the discussion of technical computer subjects?"

Recipients of the ballot were asked to check off one of three boxes:

- I believe we should discuss and argue the social responsibility of computer scientists.

- I believe we should leave this discussion to other people and stick to the discussion of technical computer subjects.

- Other views? (please express yourself freely)

Reporting on the results of the poll, Macdonald noted that as a result of raising the issue of their social responsibility, "only one reader has stated that he plans to have the laboratory [at MIT] cancel their subscription."

"Fortunately," he added, "we are sure that not many readers of the magazine agree with his viewpoint."

Macdonald wrote that he had received 217 responses to the survey, broken down as follows: "Yes, discuss" with 118 votes; "No, stick to technical subjects" with 83 votes; and "Other views (neither yes nor no indicated)" with 16 votes.

He reflected that, regardless of the outcome of the survey, he felt strongly that the magazine "clearly has a duty" to report on subjects of importance like these. The outcome of the ballot only reinforced his conviction. Macdonald made clear that discussions and arguments on the social responsibility of computer scientists would, in fact, become a vital part of the magazine's mission.

(In the same editorial forum, under the heading "Comments on 'Destruction of Civilized Existence by Automatic Computing Controls,'" an MIT scientist named Louis Sutro responded to an earlier article on the dangers of using computers to control nuclear arms deployment, concluding that, owing to the fundamental irrationality of humans, "the development of automatic computing controls, instead of precipitating a nuclear war, may help prevent it.")

Let's Get Logical

Both precedent and common sense are in favor of the thesis: computer scientists should take the initiative in pushing the social applications of computers.

—Neil Macdonald

The following month, in the May 1958 issue of **COMPUTERS AND AUTOMATION**, there appeared an extraordinary long-form article in which Macdonald explored the issue of ethical responsibility more deeply and presented his own case in more detail. The article was not-so-subtly titled "An Attempt to Apply Logic and Common Sense to the Social Responsibility of Computer Scientists."

He began by refuting the three primary arguments against computer scientists taking responsibility for their work, as culled from reader responses to the previous month's editorial.

The first argument, from which Macdonald derived the title of his article, stated that while occasional articles on the topic might be worthwhile, the subject was too often treated with "emotion and sentiment" over "logic and common sense," and therefore, the magazine should not devote too much space to the issue.

Macdonald responded by pointing out that important subjects deserve more time and attention than less important subjects. The topic of professional ethics was not only important, he believed, but it was urgent.

Furthermore, he reasoned, many of the technical advances in computing were already widely discussed and well-publicized: from their ever-increasing speed and processing capacity, to the wonder of the (then-new) "pictorial representations" of computer data on electronic displays.

What was less widely discussed and publicized, Macdonald noted, was how computers could be used to help address societal problems like unemployment and the economic recession in the United States or even "rendering accessible the enormous flood of scientific books and technical papers" being produced all around the world.

Given the incredible potential of computers to assist society in dealing with these issues, he argued, it would be both illogical and in defiance of common sense to *not* give them due attention.

Are We Underqualified?

Computer scientists … absorb the conditions of the problems they work on.

—Neil Macdonald

The second argument that Macdonald set out to refute was that computer scientists simply do not have the necessary qualifications to discuss the issue of social responsibility and that such topics should be left to social scientists.

Macdonald began by pointing out that, like mathematicians, computer scientists are often required to gain fluency in problem domains outside their area of expertise. Furthermore, he noted, expertise is not always required for criticism; in fact, attacking the credentials of a critic, rather than addressing their specific argument, is a tactic used by those who, themselves, "prefer not to be criticized."

A mathematician who specializes in statistics and probability, he argued, can certainly apply their specialized knowledge to a question involving risk mitigation, given a few days to orient themselves with regard to the problem space and get an idea of how to apply their toolset to the matter at hand.

"For after all," he concluded, "capacity to apply technique in new fields is the stock in trade of computer scientists and mathematicians."

(Ironically, this section of Macdonald's article shared the page with an advertisement by a New York company recruiting computer-savvy mathematicians to work on "hypersonic aircraft, missiles, satellites, nuclear reactors, and many other fields.")

Are We Any Different Than Ordinary Citizens?

The third argument that Macdonald set out to refute was that a computer scientist is no different than any other kind of scientist or, for that matter, an ordinary citizen, in terms of their responsibility to society; they have no more burden than anyone else.

This final refutation got to the real heart of the issue for Macdonald. He began by asking the question, "what are the special social responsibilities that computer scientists have already accepted?"

Macdonald provided a couple of examples. A computer scientist comparing the designs of two machines is socially obligated to provide an appraisal based on objective criteria and certainly would not lie to suit someone's political agenda. Therefore, a computer scientist has a social obligation to be truthful. What's more, computer scientists bear a social obligation to represent their profession with honor and dignity, and they accept that they must be honest in their work and respectful toward their employers and their customers.

Most importantly, Macdonald emphasized that the ultimate loyalty of computer scientists must be toward their fellow citizens, rather than toward a company or a government.

He explored this final point through a piece of speculative fiction, a parable involving a locksmith and a mysterious stranger.

The Story of the Locksmith

(Retold from a May 1958 editorial by Neil Macdonald published in Computers and Automation)

Once there was a locksmith, a younger man who owned his own shop and made a steady business of it. He had enough for himself and his family, but only just enough. He was known to be friendly and good-natured to his neighbors and customers.

One day, a mysterious stranger walked into the locksmith's shop. The man had a very strong presence, and his voice was high and clear. "I have a job proposition for you. There is a safe that I need opened, and it requires someone with your highly specialized skills," he said. "I've done my research and everyone seems to agree that you are the most talented locksmith in the city."

The locksmith felt very flattered and more than a little intrigued. The stranger continued.

"I'm afraid that there are certain conditions you will have to agree to as part of this job. First of all, the location of the safe must be kept secret, so you will be blindfolded as I transport you there and back. Secondly, you may not ask me anything about the safe or its contents. And finally, you can never tell anyone that I hired you."

The stranger read the confused look on the locksmith's face. "I assure you that, unusual as it is, should you take this job, I will make you rich beyond your wildest dreams."

The locksmith was excited at the proposition of such a lucrative job but also a bit nervous about not knowing anything about why the stranger needed him to open the safe. It seemed suspicious, but he thought about what the man had said about making him rich. He thought about what he might do for himself and his family with all that money.

The stranger continued, "You can have all the tools you need to do the job, too. The finest tools. I will spare no expense. If there's something you need that you don't have, I will buy it for you."

"Take your time. I'll be back tomorrow for your answer."

The locksmith tossed and turned all night, as his trepidation competed with his excitement at the prospect of a well-paying job. Finally, he made his decision. "Anyway," he thought to himself as he finally drifted off to sleep, "if I don't take this job, he'll just go to another locksmith. The second-best locksmith in the city."

The next day, when the stranger returned, the locksmith agreed to take the job.

After multiple blindfolded trips to and from the safe's unknown location, the locksmith finally managed to open it. He wasn't allowed to see what was inside of the safe: the stranger snatched its contents as soon as the lock clicked open. The stranger blindfolded the locksmith again, drove him back to his shop, and dropped him off with a briefcase full of money. True to his word, the stranger made the locksmith exceedingly rich.

A few months later, the mysterious stranger appeared on every television set in the world. He announced that he had built a superweapon that he could use to instantly destroy any living person, or even an entire city, at the touch of a button. He declared himself ruler of the earth and master of all nations.

It was later learned that the plans for this superweapon had been stolen from a very strong safe in a scientific research facility.

Was the Stranger a Criminal?

Following the story of the locksmith, Macdonald posed a series of questions, starting with whether or not the stranger was clearly a war criminal.

For the answer to this question, he turned for justification to the Nuremberg trials, a series of trials that took place after the end of World War II to determine the role of individual Nazi leaders in the terrible war crimes and atrocities they had committed.

He referred to a book titled **TYRANNY ON TRIAL: THE EVIDENCE AT NUREMBERG**, which provides a detailed report on the trials and their impact on our understanding of war crimes. He quoted the book's conclusion that killing (or the threat of killing) civilian populations in connection with war is no more excusable than killing innocent human beings under any other circumstances.

By virtue of his lethal threat against any person or persons who opposed his unilateral authority over the globe, the world's most powerful stranger was, by definition, a war criminal.

Should the Locksmith Have Known Better?

Next, Macdonald considered the question of whether the locksmith had a responsibility to evaluate the legality of what he was being asked to do.

The mysterious stranger was certainly a shady character. There were very odd conditions placed on the job: the blindfold, the unknown location, and no answer to the question of whose safe it was. Even though the stranger's purpose was not known to the locksmith, the circumstances alone should have raised a red flag. And if his questions weren't answered to his satisfaction, the locksmith was obligated to refuse the job, despite the flattery and the temptation of the pay and despite the conceit that "if I don't do the job, someone else will."

Did the Locksmith Do the Right Thing?

Macdonald made the point that not only is the mysterious stranger obviously a war criminal, but the locksmith himself is guilty as well. As the Nuremberg trials made clear, acting in accordance with someone else's orders is no ground for immunity from prosecution.

Macdonald concluded that the locksmith had not acted ethically. He had the social responsibility to determine whether the stranger was a criminal before agreeing to work with him. He must be held culpable for his neglect of his duty to society.

A War in the Editorial Section

I don't know much about morality and that, but there is this: It's always worthwhile before you do anything to consider whether it's going to hurt another person.

—John Galsworthy, 1920

In the months following the publication of the story of the locksmith, the editorial pages of **COMPUTERS AND AUTOMATION** were alive with debate. Neil Macdonald was not shy about responding and standing firm to his convictions.

A sort of editorial war was even carried out between Macdonald in **COMPUTERS AND AUTOMATION** and Charles H Johnson, editor of an industry magazine titled **JOURNAL OF MACHINE ACCOUNTING**.

Johnson had requested permission to reprint Macdonald's article and published it in the December 1958 edition of his magazine. It was presented as an excerpt in a special "The Editor Selects" section, under the heading "The Social Responsibility of Computer Scientists."

Following the awkwardly edited excerpt of the Tale of the Locksmith, Johnson wrote a rebuttal of Macdonald's premise. He called Macdonald "presumptuous in his findings" and chided him for believing that a computer scientist can in any way regulate the behavior of the rest of the world.

"The men who are responsible for warfare are not concerned with the Queensberry rules used in boxing, or rules established by the scientist, the artist, the physician or the ecclesiastic," he declared.

Johnson argued that unless computer scientists are able to guarantee that their principles of behavior could assure justice and peace, it is undesirable to place any of that responsibility in their hands at all. What's more, he continued, it's a mistake to believe that all computer scientists are even in a position to exercise their conscience, for example, those in a totalitarian state or in a repressed nation.

In the case of computer-scientist-as-locksmith, he pointed out that even an honest locksmith might be compelled to open the safe, if he believed that it was for a good cause.

He concluded with the hope that "American scientists" would continue to create for the good of their country and quoted English novelist and playwright John Galsworthy as a sort of patriotic reassurance: "Mine is that great country which shall never take toll from the weakness of others."

We Are All Locksmiths

The computer scientist, according to law and morality, does not have the right to shut his eyes in regard to the stranger, no more than the locksmith has. Both have to keep their eyes open.

—Neil Macdonald

The debate that raged through the editorial pages of these magazines continues in some form to this day and reflects the complicated questions and strong emotions arising from the question of the accountability of technologists for the work that they do.

The story of the locksmith, though a work of fiction, illustrated Macdonald's fundamental conviction that anyone with a set of specialized skills has a certain moral obligation to consider how they are used.

Macdonald explained that though the story is merely a parable, it reflected the facts of the past and present. For his real-world examples, Macdonald repeatedly turned to the ethical issues around the development of nuclear weapons. He noted that in the case of the development of a nuclear bomb, three groups of people had responsibilities akin to those of the locksmith: the atomic scientists who built the warhead, the engineers who built the propulsion mechanism, and the computer scientists who programmed the guidance systems.

Like the locksmith, Macdonald concluded, a computer scientist does have a special responsibility: "because without him, the safe cannot be opened."

Reflection

As their peers in atomic science scrambled to contain the threat of nuclear arms, early computer scientists faced their own crisis of conscience. Speculative fiction was one of the tools that helped them reason about their present-day challenges as well as explore different possible futures that lay ahead.

Just as the future history penned by H.G. Wells had shaped the thinking of an important figure in physics, Macdonald's tale of the locksmith would influence Edmund Berkeley, an important, but relatively unknown, figure in computing history.

CHAPTER 5

Machines That Think

Edmund Berkeley, the editor of **COMPUTERS AND AUTOMATION**, certainly paid attention to what Neal Macdonald was stirring up in the editorial section of his magazine. He clearly sympathized and agreed with the larger ethical principles behind Macdonald's ideas. Holding computer scientists accountable for the work that they do was a banner that Berkeley would carry forth both within his magazine and into the broader world.

Meet Edmund Berkeley

Berkeley was born in Manhattan, New York, in 1909 to a well-to-do family. His parents were both professionals, and he had a relatively uneventful childhood.

He attended a private boys' school in Manhattan for his elementary years and for high school was accepted into Phillips Exeter Academy. He graduated top of his class from Exeter in 1925 and at the age of 16 was the youngest student in his graduating class.

Like many of his classmates from Exeter, Berkeley entered Harvard University after graduation. He intended to get a degree in mining engineering but soon changed his mind and decided to pursue the creative potential of a career in mathematics instead. He began diligently studying advanced math and formal logic.

He graduated from Harvard in 1930, alongside award-winning postmodern architect Philip Johnson and two future Nobel laureates: John Franklin Enders, who is considered the "father of modern vaccines," and geneticist George Davis Snell.

© Coraline Ada Ehmke 2025
C. A. Ehmke, *We Just Build Hammers*, https://doi.org/10.1007/979-8-8688-1249-1_5

By the time Berkeley exited Harvard, the Great Depression was well underway. Although he had hoped for something a little more interesting and creative, he was forced to consider a more practical career in business, at least for the time being.

The Business of Risk

Berkeley's first exposure to computing machinery was likely in 1938, when he went to work as an actuary at Prudential Insurance.

Prudential was one of the largest insurance providers in the United States at the time. Large insurance firms like Prudential often handled up to a billion dollars in policies at once, with revenue from premiums bringing in tens of millions of dollars per year. Keeping costs low was essential to staying ahead of the intense competition in the insurance field, which led these companies to seek out ways to automate as much of their business as possible.

Tabulating technology was developed in the United States to assist in performing calculations and creating tables (thus the name) from data collected in the 1890 census. Insurance firms were the first to see its potential in the private sector. Major insurance companies, who dealt in high volumes of data, eventually came to rely on tabulation technology as a standard part of their operations.

Prudential was among the first companies to experiment with punched card tabulators in the 1890s and invested heavily for decades in the evolving state of the art. Early on in its adoption of automated tabulators, in 1895, Prudential executive John K Gore became so irritated with the limitations of existing machinery for sorting cards that he developed his own process for compiling statistics using punched cards. He hired his brother-in-law to build the machines for installation throughout Prudential's offices.

Berkeley's job as an actuary consisted of performing risk analysis and other intense and complex probabilistic computations involving large amounts of data. The work was assisted by the latest punched card tabulating machines from IBM, which, when properly maintained and operated, were capable of complex data operations at what were then remarkable speeds.

Scratching an Itch

Even with the assistance of the machines, the work was intense, challenging, and complicated. Recalling his studies at Harvard, Berkeley often wondered if it might be possible to bring the power of symbolic logic to bear in risk analysis and, in general, other probabilistic problems. He engaged with several companies involved in computing technology, including General Electric, Bell Telephone Labs, and IBM, to discuss the potential of these technologies in transforming how data processing was carried out at Prudential.

In a series of memos to company Secretary HJ Volk, Berkeley reported on his visits and conversations with these companies. The possibility of building general-purpose machines to solve data processing problems at companies like Prudential was of interest to these manufacturers. Berkeley was providing firsthand information about the data processing needs of large-scale corporations, helping them better understand the needs of a potential market.

It's likely that Berkeley's insistence that Boolean logic could be a tremendous factor in improving data processing influenced the design of the computers that emerged later that decade. But that would have to wait until after the war.

Berkeley in Wartime

In 1942, Berkeley was given leave by Prudential to join the Navy to assist in the war effort. He entered the Navy as an active-duty Reserve officer and was assigned to work on computing machinery under Howard Aiken at the Harvard Computation Laboratory.

Aiken and the Lab concentrated their efforts on the development of electromechanical computing machines that might aid the Allies in the war. Berkeley's return to his alma mater found him pursuing work on applications of Boolean algebra for programming and circuit design.

He worked alongside Aiken and fellow Navy officer Grace Hopper on the operation of the Harvard Mark I, an early general-purpose computing device. The Mark I's construction had been authorized in 1939, so the Mark I was not technically built specifically for military use. However, following a demonstration of the machine in 1944, John von Neumann did in fact use the Mark I to perform some calculations related to his work in Los Alamos on the Manhattan Project.

Berkeley found Aiken's mannerisms grating, and the two maintained a tense and not always civil relationship. At one point, Berkeley is said to have gotten so frustrated with Aiken's temperament that suggested to his superior that he read **How to Win Friends and Influence People**.

Regardless, he found the work challenging and rewarding of its own accord, and he likely found satisfaction in being able to fully put his mathematical creativity to use.

A Return to Civilian Life

I think it is safe to say that we are at the threshold of a new development that will reduce materially the present clerical work going on in life insurance companies. It will transform the numerical work for many actuarial calculations, and enable actuaries to do many things they now only dream of doing.

—Edmund Berkeley, "Electronic Machinery for Handling Information, and Its Uses in Insurance," 1947

Although Berkeley had nominally been in the Navy during World War II, to work on a computer that played a part in wartime research, following the war, he found no interest in continuing to work for the military and returned to civilian life.

Newly energized by the technology he had worked with at the Harvard Computation Lab, Berkeley returned to Prudential in 1946 as an analyst. He soon worked his way up to Chief Research Consultant, where his primary responsibility was investigating the use of advanced computing machinery to improve data processing at the company.

His experience working on the Mark I and Mark II computers only redoubled his dream of the technology representing the future of data processing. He pursued an even more aggressive schedule of meetings with manufacturers, reportedly conducting almost 60 meetings between August and December of 1946.

Frustrated with waiting for the industry to catch up with his imagination, Berkeley wrote a detailed specification of Prudential's particular computing needs. Titled "Sequence Controlled Calculators for the Prudential—Specifications," it laid out a list of requirements for new electronic computers and concluded with an insistence on close collaboration between engineers from the manufacturer and employees of Prudential.

Building to Spec

The specification caught the attention of multiple manufacturers, including Raytheon, the Eckert–Mauchly Computer Corporation, and IBM. One vendor took Berkeley's suggestion to work hand in hand with Prudential at all stages of design and construction to heart, proposing to work with a consortium of insurance companies to build specifically to industry needs.

All of the vendor proposals were appealing to Berkeley, with the exception of IBM's. He felt that the inertia of IBM's heavy investment in tabulating machines would prove to be an obstacle to serious pursuit of an alternative technology. What's more, he had seen for himself the friction that existed between IBM and the Harvard Computation Lab during the war years, which led to the cancellation of IBM's involvement in the Mark I project. His argument against the IBM proposal was so persuasive that Prudential actually began scaling back its investment in IBM stock.

The following year, in 1947, Eckert–Mauchly won the contract with Prudential. They agreed to build a machine that fulfilled as many of the specs as possible—barring certain unrealistic requirements that Berkeley had, such as the capability for unsupervised overnight operation. The amount of the contract was the equivalent to about half of Prudential's annual rental fees to IBM for its tabulating machines.

Most importantly, the contract with Prudential led Eckert–Mauchly to develop the UNIVAC, the world's first general-purpose digital computer, with engineers and computer scientists hired from the Moore School of Electrical Engineering at the University of Pennsylvania, where the ENIAC computer was developed just two years earlier.

The Association for Computing Machinery

We believe there is ample interest to start an informal associa-
tion of many of those interested in the new machinery for
computing and reasoning. Since there has to be a beginning,
we are acting as a temporary committee to start such an
association.

—Edmund Berkeley

Berkeley was not alone in his fixation on the future of computing machinery. There was growing interest across industries and fields, with large and enthusiastic attendance at various meetings and seminars across the country.

On June 24, 1947, he wrote an open letter, sent to various colleagues and associates, on behalf of a founding committee of eight of his fellow computer scientists. This committee included representatives from Raytheon, the United States Bureau of Standards, the Office of Naval Research, and the Moore School of Electrical Engineering. The letter proposed an informal organization for computer scientists on the East Coast of the United States.

Berkeley had hoped for someone with more influence in the nascent computer industry to cosign the letter. He approached several prominent practitioners in computing, including his former boss at Harvard Lab, Howard Aiken. Aiken rebuffed Berkeley's invitation, responding that computing was simply a branch of mathematics, and didn't warrant its own organization. Berkeley received similar rebukes from other scientists working in computing. John von Neumann is said to have remarked, "Oh, for Heaven's sake, not another association!"

The letter highlighted particular centers of interest in computing in Boston, New York, Princeton, Philadelphia, Aberdeen, and Washington, DC, so it was decided that the organization would be called the Eastern Association for Computing Machinery. The letter also kept open the possibility of converting to a more formal organization should there be a sufficient interest.

By January of 1948, a short six months later, it was clear that there was wider geographical interest in the organization. The word "Eastern" was dropped from its name.

The organization's stated purpose was to "advance the science, development, construction, and application of the new machinery for computing, reasoning, and other handling of information." The letter proposed regular quarterly meetings in Boston, New York, and Philadelphia, at which local committees could conduct their business and members could present short reports or papers on recent developments for discussion. The organization was not going to publish its own papers, but would circulate those of its members via mimeographed copies mailed out to a list of interested persons.

Almost all of the eight founders of the ACM gained their experience with computing machinery as part of the war effort, but most of them had left the military behind and returned to civilian careers.

The ACM was the first professional organization of computer engineers and scientists. Today, it is the largest nonprofit organization for computing in the world, boasting over 100,000 members, with the charter to "foster the open interchange of information and promote the highest professional and ethical standards" in the field of computer science.

Computers and Automation

Even at the earliest stages in the development of the nascent computer industry, Berkeley was aware of the tremendous potential of computers to contribute to the welfare of the world or to cause great harm to society. He knew firsthand, from his work at Harvard Lab, that the military implications of computing were enormous. His work to secure a footing for new computing machines in the civilian world created a different set of incentives.

Perhaps inspired by the atomic scientists who, following the horrors of the atomic bomb, established the **BULLETIN OF THE ATOMIC SCIENTIST**, Berkeley founded the first magazine for computing in 1951.

As the mission of the magazine evolved over time, it underwent several name changes, from the unwieldy **ROSTER OF ORGANIZATIONS IN THE FIELD OF AUTOMATIC COMPUTING MACHINERY** to **THE COMPUTING MACHINERY FIELD**, **COMPUTERS AND AUTOMATION**, and finally, in 1975, **COMPUTERS AND PEOPLE**. Each iteration of the name reflected the changing paradigm of computing over two decades.

By 1954, the magazine was being published monthly, with an annual subscription cost of just under USD$5.

On a page in the back of the magazine, there was always a form that could be cut out, filled in, and mailed back to the magazine, postage paid. This would ensure the sender's inclusion in a list of "Who's Who" of computing. In addition to standard biographical information, respondents were asked to specify the year that they entered the computing field and to indicate their primary interests from a list including computer design, construction, applications, sales, electronics, mathematics, and business uses. Readers were encouraged to provide as much additional information of interest about themselves as they desired. The Who's Who was published twice a year in the form of a supplement in a special edition of the magazine.

Advertisers in the magazine, including Remington Rand, Sylvania, Honeywell, and General Electric, were politely reminded that their adverts should conform to the stated purpose of **COMPUTERS AND AUTOMATION**: to be factual, useful, and understandable.

The magazine always retained its technical focus and its celebratory attitude toward the rapid advances taking place in the industry. But the social and political tensions of the broader world were also increasingly reflected in its pages. Berkeley was unwavering in his support of assistant editor Neil Macdonald's efforts to bring accountability and responsibility to the field. He was glad to see the magazine used as a platform for this ethical campaign.

The Computing of Art

We may say most aptly that the Analytical Engine weaves algebraical patterns just as the Jacquard-loom weaves flowers and leaves.

—Ada Lovelace, 1843

The January 1963 issue of **COMPUTERS AND AUTOMATION** bore a color image that was as striking as it was mysterious.

Under a caption that read "A Portrait by a Computer As a Young Artist," the image consisted of thin horizontal stripes of bright red lines, standing out crisply from a black background. With an almost three-dimensional effect, some of the lines formed waves of elegant vertical curves, a digital topography, almost like shapes rising from a horizontal plane.

An explanation of the curious image appeared in the "Readers' and Editors' Forum" of the magazine. The article began poetically: "The brush is an electron beam; the canvas, an oscilloscope; the painter, an electronic computer. The result: an intriguing form of 'electronic surrealism.'" The editor goes on to describe the curved shapes as "phosphorescent stalagmites."

The artist was Ebram Arazi, a student at MIT. He created the image as part of his "Art for Engineers" coursework. The image was created by pointing a scanning camera, not unlike the television cameras of the time, at circles of light made by shining a lamp through a metal plate drilled through with overlapping, randomly sized and randomly positioned holes. The scan lines of the camera were then read as a series of x and y coordinates, with a third value, I, representing the intensity or brightness of each point along the line. These values were displayed as x and y + I coordinates on an oscilloscope, and its display was then photographed.

The student was quoted as saying that he wanted to extend the idea, perhaps using the computer to control an automated milling machine to recreate the image as a three-dimensional shape carved from a block of metal. This way, he added, the computer could be "a sculptor as well as a painter."

The image is one of the first examples of what we today consider computer art. The following issue, for February 1963, announced the magazine's new "Computer Art Contest," described as an informal competition "for visual creativity in which a computer plays a dominant role."

Thus, the term "computer art" was coined by Berkeley with his friend Grace C Hertlein, an acclaimed Chicago-based artist, musician, and teacher. Hertlein judged the computer art contest each year following and even founded her own magazine, **COMPUTER GRAPHICS AND ART**, in 1976.

Machines That Think

Along with the release of atomic energy, [computers] are one of the great achievements of the present century. No one can afford to be unaware of their significance.

—Edmund Berkeley

In 1949, Berkeley published **GIANT BRAINS, OR MACHINES THAT THINK**, the first book on electronic computers written for a general audience.

The book was intended to be read in a nonlinear fashion, with the reader jumping between topics of interest and a supplement in the back of the book containing clear explanations of different mathematical operations they may not have already known about. There were sections describing how to convert between decimal and binary numbers, explaining basic algebraic concepts, and even going as far as trigonometry and matrix math.

Another supplement in the back of the book provided page after page of references the reader could follow up on to deepen their understanding of fundamental concepts from the book. These references were divided by subject area, with lists of books about the human brain, linguistics, and a host of specific examples of real-world computers.

In one chapter, Berkeley expounded the types of problems that computers might solve in the future. He foresaw their use in meteorology, and described a so-called "weather brain" that collects data from thousands of weather observatories. The computer then processes that data to produce weather forecasts. Berkeley also predicted the future use of computers in intelligence and aptitude testing.

Later in the book, he devoted an entire chapter to exploring the societal implications of computers. "It is not right nor proper for a scientist," he admonished, "to have no regard for what his discoveries may lead to." Berkeley called back to Mary Wollstonecraft Shelley's **FRANKENSTEIN** as an example of what terrible consequences can occur when a scientist loses control of "a machine that thinks."

GIANT BRAINS, OR MACHINES THAT THINK is sometimes credited with popularizing the metaphor of a computer as a brain, although H.G. Wells's 1939 **WORLD BRAIN**, which basically described today's Wikipedia, probably originated the idea. In fact, Well's description of a "world brain" may even have influenced Berkeley's conception of the promise of computers.

Simon

We shall now consider how we can design a very simple machine that will think. Let us call it Simon.

—Edmund Berkeley, **GIANT BRAINS, OR MACHINES THAT THINK**, 1949

One of the most interesting chapters in **GIANT BRAINS** explained the construction of a relatively simple computer called Simon, after the childhood rhyme of "Simple Simon." The machine could be built for around US$300 in parts, or approximately $3,500 in 2024 US dollars.

After a demonstration of Simon by Berkeley at Columbia University, a "fact sheet" was circulated that described Simon as "the smallest complete mechanical brain in existence." The first working version of Simon was built by William Porter, a mechanical engineer who had helped construct the Harvard Mark II and Mark III calculators. He was assisted by two graduate students in the electrical engineering program at the university. The trio made some improvements and modifications on Berkeley's original design, including an error-handling mechanism and a redesigned power supply. The device weighed less than 40 pounds and was about the size and shape of a grocery delivery box.

Berkeley was comically dismissive of Simon's computing power, saying it was "almost a moron" and that it would make anyone in the room feel smart. Simon wasn't designed to show off the intelligence of computers. Rather, it was intended to be a teaching device for young people, to demystify the technology and inspire a new generation of computer scientists.

Berkeley hoped that it would spark an interest in building computers like the popular hobby of building crystal radio sets in the decade before. By 1959, he had sold nearly 500 Simon kits. He even included his Simon computer in the "Roster of Automatic Computers" directory published annually in **COMPUTERS AND AUTOMATION**.

Simon was capable of addition, negation (subtraction from zero), greater-than comparisons, and simple if/then logic. It had only two bits of memory, meaning that it could only express the numbers 0, 1, 2, and 3. Berkeley described a simple program that Simon could execute: "Add 2 and 1; find the negative of 3; find whether the first result is greater than the second; if so, select 2; if not, select 3." Simon could process 200 instructions like these. It read the program from paper tape and displayed program output through five lamps on its console.

The idea of a computer that could be built and operated at home was revolutionary, and many credit Berkeley with essentially having predicted the advent of home computers some decades later.

The popular press loved the novelty of Berkeley's "tiny brains." He was even the subject of a photo spread in LIFE magazine.

At the conclusion of a cover story on Simon in **SCIENTIFIC AMERICAN** in 1950, Berkeley was asked to describe his hopes for Simon's future. He responded, "It may stimulate thought and discussion on the philosophical and social implications of machines that handle information."

Small Robots

Make your own tiny genius computers!

—From an ad for Geniac, published in **COMPUTERS & AUTOMATION**, September 1956

Encouraged by the success of Simon, Berkeley set out to create a menagerie of computers for teaching and learning.

The first successor to Simon was the "Geniac," an educational toy that was capable of being rewired to create "machines" capable not only of mathematical operations, but acting as a decoder ring, playing simple games, and solving logical syllogisms. Programming the Geniac involved rewiring the machine's simple "multiple switch," a perforated ceramic disk to which wires could be attached without the need for soldering.

One such program for the Geniac was a "machine' for determining the gender of a test subject. The user was instructed to answer five questions, including deciding between a toy train and a doll as an ideal present for themselves.

Berkeley sold other single-problem computers (what he called "Small Robots") to demonstrate different computing principles. One of them was called "R1: Douglas Macdonald's Will." The instructions described the provisions of a fictional father's will:

If my son Angus survives me and my son Brian does not, all my estate goes to Angus. If Brian survives me and Angus does not, all my estate goes to Brian. If neither survives me, my estate is to go to the Gaelic Home for the Aged and Indigent. If both Angus and Brian survive me, and if at the time of my death neither is married nor is a graduate of Edinburgh University, then each shall have 50% of my estate. If both are married and neither is a graduate, or if both are graduates and neither is married, or if both are graduates and both are married, then each shall have 50% of my estate. If only one of my sons is a graduate, his share shall be increased by 20% of my estate, and the other's decreased accordingly. If only one of my sons is married, his share shall be increased by 10% of my estate, and the other is decreased accordingly.

After establishing the conditions of Angus and Brian using a series of switches as input, the answer to the question of what happens when Douglas Macdonald dies was displayed using a series of ten bulbs.

These single-problem computers ran on a flashlight battery and sold for just under $50.

Berkeley continued producing his "machines that think" for decades to come and through his magazine and his work tried to make the technology accessible, teachable, and fun.

Reflection

Edmund Berkeley saw very early in the computing industry's history that "computer people" carried a heavier-than-average burden. He believed that they bore responsibility for how their work was being used, for social good or social ill. His life's work was to try to tip the scales in humanity's favor. But did his peers share his vision for the future of ethical computing?

CHAPTER 6

Machines That Kill

Not all of Edmund Berkeley's peers took the same position on social responsibility that he did. In light of what he saw as their disregard for the societal consequences of the technology they were developing, Berkeley would have to become the conscience of the computing field. And, as we will see, this often put him in conflict with prominent figures in his field.

Cooperation in Horror

> *It is often easier for a scientist to study his science than to study the results for good or evil that his discoveries may lead to. But it is not right nor proper for a scientist, a man who is loyal to truth as an ideal, to have no regard for what his discoveries may lead to.*

—Edmund Berkeley

Berkeley saw how technology was used for direct warfare, like the technology behind the atomic bomb or the Nazis' guided bombs, but also its role in human rights atrocities against civilians. Computing technology was no different. After the war, it was learned that the Nazis used early mechanical computing devices, bought from IBM's German subsidiary, to collect census data that would later be used to organize roundups as part of the Holocaust. Punch cards from the IBM tabulation machines were even sent along with the trains transporting victims to concentration camps.

© Coraline Ada Ehmke 2025
C. A. Ehmke, *We Just Build Hammers*, https://doi.org/10.1007/979-8-8688-1249-1_6

Despite his strong feelings about how computers were being used by the military, Berkeley did not have a simplistic or knee-jerk antimilitary attitude. He understood that nations have a need for a standing military for defensive purposes. Berkeley did not regret his time serving in the Navy during the war, and in fact, he remained in the Navy Reserves for some years after the war.

But he made a differentiation between technologies that were used primarily for defense, such as radar and communications devices, and those that were specifically designed to kill and maim, such as long-range missiles and antipersonnel weapons.

His distinction between defense and atrocity was made clear in the February 1958 issue of **COMPUTERS AND AUTOMATION**, when Berkeley used his voice in the editorial section of the magazine to discuss a recent article that had been submitted for publishing consideration.

The article had to do with a novel way of using computers to perform complex diffusion calculations, to model the behavior of various gasses as they move from areas of high concentration to areas of low concentration. The math was fascinating, but Berkeley noticed something: the author of the article worked for the US Army Chemical Corps.

He continued reading. While the author didn't use the specific term "poison gas," it became increasingly obvious from the description of the problem that the diffusion that was being studied was that of a chemical weapon.

Berkeley's rage came through in his scathing public rejection of the article. He wrote, "Is there no point at which a self-respecting human being should say, 'I cannot do this, I cannot study this, investigate this, publish this ... I cannot have anything to do with this. This is horrible.'?"

He characterized the author's work as a "cooperation in horror." Berkeley made the comparison to wartime Germany, postulating that with the same technology, the Nazis could have been much more efficient in calculating exactly how much poison gas would be required to kill various numbers of Jewish prisoners in concentration camps. He noted that even torture was a field that was open to science.

Berkeley concluded by stating that "it will be a very long time if ever" before **Computers and Automation** would publish articles dealing so coldly and dispassionately with issues of death and destruction.

Saving the World from Itself

Most problems have either many answers or no answer. Only a few problems have one.

—Edmund Berkeley

Berkeley could easily imagine the best and worst possible outcomes of rapidly advancing computing technologies. And just as Szilard and his allies were doing in the field of atomic science, Berkeley tried to orchestrate ethical constraints in his own field of computer science. He frequently cited the work of atomic scientists as positive examples of responsible technology and drew inspiration from their methods.

In his book **Giant Brains, or Machines that Think**, Berkeley devoted an entire chapter to what he called the "social control" of computers. He anticipated the "simply a tool" argument and sidestepped it gracefully by focusing on the kinds of problems that computers were being designed to solve. Machines are constructed for the reason of their use, he reasoned, so a machine and its uses were inseparable.

He placed due responsibility on computer scientists, whom he believed could behave more rationally than the governments, militaries, and corporations that employed them. He hoped that they might act more as benefactors to humanity or "trustees of our human inheritance." Acting otherwise meant behaving like a drone that enjoyed the benefits of being part of the hive while doing none of the work to earn its keep.

Frankenstein and the Robots

The more minds that go to work on solving the problem of social control over robot machines and other products of the new technology—which is rushing upon us from the discoveries of the scientists—the better off we all will be.

—Edmund Berkeley

In the chapter on social control, Berkeley continued by citing two cautionary tales, both works of fiction, as parables warning against simply hoping for the best and letting the course of events happen as they come.

The first was the tale of **FRANKENSTEIN**, written in 1818 by then-21-year-old Mary Wollstonecraft Shelley. In the book, after discovering the secret of life, a young scientist creates an intelligent and clever being, imbued with a soul, but embodied in a terror-inducing, monstrous form. Victor Frankenstein's own horror toward the creature causes him to reject his responsibility as its creator, resulting in death and ruin for everyone he loved and leaving a trail of blood from the Swiss Alps to the Arctic Circle.

The second tale came from a Czech play from the 1920s, called **ROSSUM'S UNIVERSAL ROBOTS**. The protagonist is a scientist who, like Frankenstein, discovers the organizing principles of living matter and uses this knowledge to manufacture hundreds of "robata," or artificial servants. These creatures serve as a labor force, a fighting force, and in any other role imagined by those wealthy enough to purchase them.

Their creator anticipates that the robata will eliminate the need for workers, freeing people from "the degradation of labor" and making poverty a thing of the past. He imagines a world like the one described by Wells in **THE WORLD SET FREE**: a world in which the only responsibility that people have is for their own betterment. The story, however, does not end on such a happy note; the creatures develop emotions, and the capacity for pain, and come to see humanity as their oppressor and enemy.

Berkeley noted that both the Frankenstein and Robata stories are prophetic and perfectly illustrate how creators can be destroyed by losing control of their creations.

Means of Exercising Social Control

It is the nature of control to put a fence around danger.

—Edmund Berkeley

Berkeley anticipated two main threats that computers posed toward humanity: the threat of physical harm and the threat of economic harm.

The computers that existed after the war were as far removed from the early days of tabulating machines as humans were from their own primitive ancestors. Their potential for facilitating physical harm was the main motivation for the rapid development of novel computing machines during wartime. And that investment continued even after the war; after all, the majority of Berkeley's peers and colleagues had stayed on with the military to continue to develop new generations of killing machines, capable of even greater destruction.

In terms of economic harm, Berkeley imagined the upheaval of labor caused by the automation of an earlier industrial revolution magnified tenfold. He pictured factories that, once constructed, were so efficiently operated by computer-controlled machinery that they would require perhaps one or two humans to be employed as overseers and for maintenance; once such a factory was ready to begin producing goods, there would be little need for further human intervention. This arrangement, however, would raise the issue of rendering labor, skill, and expertise obsolete. In turn, this would lead to businesses trying to sell their efficiently manufactured goods to a population rendered destitute by mass unemployment.

To stave off these threats, Berkeley conceived a scheme for the "social control" of computers. Social control would ensure that the advantages of computer-controlled automation were evenly distributed to everyone. He laid out two strategies for realizing social control: one for an idealized world of rational and principled actors and one for the messier, irrational world in which we actually live.

A More Rational World

The struggle of this century, it seems to me, is a struggle of ideas. It looks as if no war can be won any more with guns or bombs or any hardware, but only with ideas.

—Edmund Berkeley, 1955

Like many scientists before and after him, Berkeley was frequently frustrated by the fundamental irrationality of his fellow human beings. In a rational world, he argued, only two fundamental instruments of social control need be employed to ensure that computing technology would live up to its prosocial potential: political systems and economic systems.

He envisioned a society in which regulations would constrain the profit-motivated ambitions of corporations that used computers, ensuring the safety and well-being of the population impacted by their use. He drew comparisons to privatized endeavors like air travel, which operated safely in large part due to regulatory measures designed and enforced by the public through its governing bodies. Berkeley believed that with a similar system of checks and balances between public and private interests, evolving computer technologies would be easier to control and safer to the world.

Further, some classes of work by computers would need to be solely under governmental control. For example, it would be disastrous for technologies for developing atomic bombs, long-range missiles, and other weapons to fall outside the control of legitimate governments and into the hands of agents like Macdonald's mysterious stranger.

Like Wells, Berkeley also saw a role for international oversight. He reasoned that there would have to be some sort of global agency established, perhaps under the control of the United Nations, to inspect and investigate how computers were being designed and used around the world. This ensured that state actors were operating in accordance with global principles of peace and public good.

As far as the problem of poverty through labor replacement was concerned, Berkeley took a decidedly socialist position. He called for a system for distribution of wealth that would incentivize continued research and development of new technologies while also providing for a population that was freed from employment and provided with all that it needed or desired.

Navigating the Irrational

As soon as antisocial human beings have access to the controls, the danger to society becomes great.

—Edmund Berkeley

Berkeley believed that if only rationality would prevail, the people of the world could be saved from themselves and freed from the danger of the technologies that they unleashed.

But he also knew, of course, that the world we live in is far from rational. Corporations are motivated by maximizing profits over any obligation to social good. Checks and balances between public and private interests are tainted by dishonesty, greed, and a desire for control. Militaries exist for the violent defense of one nation's interests against that of its neighbors. Governments are human institutions that reflect human flaws. He saw little evidence of rationality in any of these social controls.

Berkeley identified three primary obstacles to reasonable and effective social control: ignorance, prejudice, and a "narrow point of view."

He considered ignorance to be a lack of sophisticated knowledge, not a stubborn refutation of truth. In this regard, a lack of understanding of computers and their potential for good or harm would be exacerbated by reserving such knowledge for scientists alone. The more that the public understood about computers and how they worked, the less chance there would be of catastrophe. And computers themselves might even be used as teachers to educate the masses. Berkeley promoted this educational approach through his computer kits and "small robots."

Prejudice would prove a more substantial obstacle. Berkeley saw prejudice as a natural phenomenon emerging from an emphasis on systems of belief over systems of knowledge. He described the difficulty that humans have with sorting out beliefs from verifiable, objective facts. Taking a scientific approach to a problem like this could, he reasoned, bring an end to violence, racism, intolerance, and other aggressive manifestations of prejudice.

Finally, Berkeley believed that the root of both ignorance and prejudice came down to the human propensity for maintaining a narrow, uninformed, and purely self-interested attitude. The problem of control over technology must have no national boundaries, must hold no loyalty to a single country, and must be built on the "old and fine tradition" of scientific inquiry into truth.

Report on the Social Responsibilities of Computer People

And if a single computer scientist has trouble thinking all this out logically, then let's have a committee of computer scientists to get together and think this out, and study the social responsibility of computer scientists, with due regard to objective evidence, the toughest of sound logic, and the most practical of common sense.

—Neil Macdonald, **Computers and Automation**,
May 1958

In 1958, within the pages of **COMPUTERS AND AUTOMATION**, Neil Macdonald had suggested that a committee be formed to investigate to what extent computer scientists were responsible for their creations, and Edmund Berkeley set out to make that happen.

With three of his colleagues and fellow members of the Association for Computing Machinery, Berkeley petitioned the Council of the ACM at its June meeting to establish the Committee on the Social Responsibilities of Computer People. The proposed committee had four members: Edmund Berkeley; Saul Gorn, who taught at the Moore School; Melvin A. Shader from IBM; and Arvid W. Jacobson, a former Communist spy who was now leading computer research projects at Wayne University.

The committee was charged with investigating "the social responsibilities of computer people to advance socially desirable applications of computers and to help prevent socially undesirable applications."

The Council voted to approve the committee, and Berkeley and his colleagues met three times before submitting their report in December 1958. The Council accepted the report and voted to keep the committee active and to establish a procedure "whereby the ACM may officially take cognizance of serious issues in the important area of professional, ethical, and social questions arising among its members."

The report was published in full in **COMPUTERS AND AUTOMATION** the following February. In its preamble, it is stated that "man's power has increased a thousand-fold. Compare the ancient man with his bow and arrow to today's pilot carrying atom bombs. Thus the individual has acquired power to effect drastic changes in the conditions of life of many people." This relates to Wells's conception of power as a sort of human industriousness inseparable from coevolving technologies.

"Since computers are inextricably tied to economy and culture," the report continued, "we must never lose sight of their importance to the welfare of our country and mankind."

The committee came to the conclusion that, given the incredible potential of computers for broad good as well as broad harm, ethical considerations were paramount.

The Four Ethical Responsibilities

In the report, the committee laid out what they saw as the four primary ethical responsibilities of computer scientists toward society, their profession, their employers, their country, and, most importantly, to humanity as a whole:

- He [sic] cannot rightly ignore his ethical responsibilities.

- He cannot rightly delegate his ethical responsibilities. Therefore, he should not accept, without thinking, standards of values and behavior suggested to him.

- He cannot rightly neglect to think about how his special role as a computer person can benefit or harm society.

- He cannot rightly avoid deciding between conflicting ethical responsibilities. Therefore, he must think how to choose.

The report declared that in a conflict between value systems, such as "the advancement of pure knowledge" being in conflict with "science in the service of humanity," individuals have a responsibility to make a conscious choice, one that cannot be delegated to anyone else.

Argument of the Beard

The work to promote social responsibility among computer technologists was often met with resistance related to ethical "gray areas" that can make it difficult to distinguish between positive and negative uses and potentials—a refutation of black-and-white thinking.

This recalls arguments that Macdonald had previously made, in critiquing attempts to sidestep important conversations by arguing over hypothetical exceptions that were realistically insignificant. This was a refutation of a logical fallacy called the "Argument of the Beard" or the "Paradox of Small Differences." As it is usually described, the fallacy posits the question of how many hairs on a man's face constitute a beard. If it is agreed that 1,000 whiskers make up a beard, why not 999? Why not 500? Why not 100? Why not 50? At which specific point is a beard no longer a beard?

According to the book **APPLIED LOGIC** by W. W. Little, W. H. Wilson, and W. E. Moore, the argument of the beard presents a fallacy that is the polar opposite of simplistic, binary thinking. It meets the simplicity of black-and-white thinking with a continuous shaded middle ground that renders differences between polar opposites impossible to distinguish. As the authors put it, "The fact that we cannot determine the exact point at which white ceases to be white does not prove that there is no difference between white and black."

The report met the gray area criticism with the simple statement that "given the ethical value system we are using in our century, we can label some classes of work as obviously socially desirable, and other classes of work as obviously socially undesirable, even if there is a large middle ground which cannot be clearly classified."

Following the publication of the report, Berkeley continued to be inspired by Macdonald's work and collaborated in expanding the scope of the magazine to cover what today might be called the techno-social aspects of computers.

Berkeley in the Age of McCarthy

As to social, political, and/or religious views, I have some strong convictions. But as a result of Mr. Joe McCarthy and some other people who promote 'guilt by association,' I don't speak out as freely as I used to.

—Edmund Berkeley, quoted in the **Harvard Class of 1930 25th Anniversary Report**

Berkeley found that his politics were increasingly at odds with his peers in the industry. What's more, the politics of his early career were also coming under scrutiny by a society obsessed with the threat of communist infiltrators and sympathizers.

Eckert–Mauchly, the company which had taken Berkeley's specifications and built the UNIVAC for Prudential, was accused of having hired engineers with "communist leanings" and lost its contracts and clearance for military work.

Berkeley found himself the subject of an investigation by the Navy in 1955. He had retained his rank in the Naval Reserve post-war, but that commission was now threatened by accusations of leftist sympathies dating back to his antifascist activism in the 1930s. Eventually, Berkeley was deemed a security risk and given the opportunity to resign with an honorable discharge.

Even his work with the ACM came under scrutiny. With regard to the findings of the Committee on Social Responsibilities, a colleague called out Berkeley as being dishonest and disingenuous in the matter by not disclosing his political affiliations in the context of the committee's findings.

Throughout, Berkeley denied any communist leanings and spoke out about his real views on communism, but the "guilt by association" he spoke of in his Harvard autobiographical note haunted him for decades to come. Berkeley found this stigma frustrating, simplistic, and irrational.

He wrote, "Before Americans can make rational judgments about the rest of the world [...] they have to study more perceptively and blow their mouths off less."

The ACM 25th Anniversary Gala

I think what the ACM should concentrate on is making a list of the nine most important problems in the world. And then if they have time left over, publish the junk that only 50 people can understand.

—Edmund Berkeley, 1987

Berkeley's politics were also troubling to his colleagues at the Association for Computing Machinery. According to Berkeley biographer Bernadette Longo, the organization had an informal policy of distancing itself from Berkeley to the point where even his founding role had been downplayed and obscured for decades.

Things came to a head in 1972 when the seven surviving founders of the ACM received invitations to a celebration in Boston with cocktails, dinner, and speeches to mark the organization's 25th anniversary. Walter Carlson, who was president of the organization at the time, was uncertain about even inviting Berkeley, let alone letting him share remarks, but finally decided to ask Berkeley if he would be interested in addressing the attendees of the celebration dinner.

This event was just one among many at the ACM's annual conference that year. The conference saw record attendance, with nearly 1,500 people attending various talks, panel discussions, and technology demonstrations. One of the highlights of the conference was a standing-room only computer chess tournament, moderated by a Scottish chess master flown in for the occasion by the organizers.

The 100 invitees to the gala were selected carefully and included prominent members and chapter leaders from across the country and from as far away as the Netherlands.

Berkeley followed early ACM president Franz Alt with a talk titled "Horizons," which was supposed to be about the future of computing. But the speech was fiery and confrontational instead. Berkeley had campaigned for ethical standards in the computer industry for 20 years, but his ideas never seemed to gain traction. His frustration or even anger with his colleagues had finally become too much to contain.

The hostility toward his work, from the committee's report, the discussions in his magazine, and other efforts by Berkeley throughout the 1950s and 1960s had failed to move his fellow computer scientists to action. So it was a very frustrated Edmund Berkeley who addressed the gathering, and he called down righteous fury on his peers that August night in 1972.

No copy of his speech is known to have been preserved, but a week later, a summary was printed on the front page of **COMPUTERWORLD** magazine under the headline "Founder Hits Social Role: ACM Blasted for 'Neglect.'" The article quotes Berkeley as saying that it was a "gross neglect of responsibility" that the ACM refused to prioritize the social good or ill of computer applications.

During his speech, Berkeley declared that, without the intervention of social science in the field of computing, humanity would be extinct within 500 years, from a combination of war and climate disaster. The flames of humanity's destruction would be supported by corporations resisting efforts to combat it, because they profited from it.

Berkeley called for an "Association for the Prevention of Doomsday" and coined the term "atrocity engineering" to refer to the development of computers for military use. He called out his fellow computer scientists working for Honeywell in designing antipersonnel bombs for use in Vietnam as an example.

He went on to tell the audience that anyone present whose work promoted unethical use of computers, including their use in developing weapons technology, should immediately quit their jobs. He called out members of the audience by name. People who worked directly for the military. People who worked as subcontractors. People who worked in university research labs.

It was a shock to the staid and esteemed professionals who were assembled there that night. Many of his peers, including his former Navy colleague Grace Hopper, were so upset by his accusations that they stood up and walked out in the middle of his speech.

According to a publication by the IEEE Computer History Committee, ACM leaders were embarrassed by their honoree, and the organization never publicly acknowledged the speech, let alone addressed any of its criticisms.

Ride the East Wind

Most good stories imply more than one conclusion.

—Edmund Berkeley, *Ride the East Wind*

Like Leo Szilard before him with his **VOICE OF THE DOLPHINS**, Berkeley turned to fiction in his twilight years to reflect upon and relate his values in a more digestible form. Frustrated with the irrationality and lack of moral character surrounding him in the world, he decided to use parables as the instrument of his moral explorations.

Berkeley published nearly a dozen books in his lifetime, and one of his last consisted of retellings of classic parables and fables, mixed with a few of his own devising. Published in 1973, **RIDE THE EAST WIND** presented 50 stories from writers and thinkers like Aesop, Hans Christian Andersen, Benjamin Franklin, and Isaac Newton.

In the book, Berkeley provided modern takes on each of the morality lessons in the selected stories, referring to his observations, interpretations, and related quotes from other thinkers as "bouquets" of distilled wisdom. For example, at the conclusion of the story of Pandora's Box, Berkeley quoted Scottish philosopher Thomas Carlyle's observation that "Man has no other possession but Hope."

One fable, penned by Berkeley himself and titled "The Fire Squirrels," involves two squirrels discussing natural history around a campfire. One squirrel tells the other about the fate of a now-extinct species, *Homo sapiens*, which pursued weapons of destruction that led to their own extinction, which was not unusual for a race of creatures that is the first to inhabit a novel "corridor" of nature. In this case, the niche that humanity had found itself in was the intersection of language and toolmaking. But, the squirrel declares, humans were so stunted emotionally that they could think of no better use for these anomalous skills than self-destruction. After the conclusion of the fable, among the other "flowers" in the critical bouquet, Berkeley summarized the tale of humanity with the observation that "thoughtless technology is a curse."

Interestingly, Berkeley's book also included his associate editor Neil Macdonald's parable under the title "The Locksmith and the Stranger." He summed up the story with resignation that calls back to his frustration with his peers in the computing industry: "It is not comforting to know that your skills and your work have forged a link in a chain of evil."

Berkeley's Legacy

What has to be taught about computers results from looking at the world and seeing what needs to be taught about computers.

—Edmund Berkeley

Edmund Berkeley died of liver cancer on March 7, 1988. Despite the computer industry embarrassedly sweeping his words and his work under the carpet, he remains an important figure in the history of computing. Berkeley never shied away from the truth and stuck to his convictions to his dying day.

As he prepared to write his friend's obituary, Eric Weiss wrote to other friends and colleagues of Berkeley's to gather anecdotes and observations about the man. It was then that the truth about the relationship between Edmund Berkeley and his apparent moral inspiration Neil Macdonald was finally revealed. They were, in fact, the same person: writing under Macdonald's name began as a trick to disguise the fact that Berkeley produced his magazine "almost single-handedly."

Weiss later reflected that Berkeley's "use of a pseudonymous associate editor and the inward chuckle that surely it gave Ed" was an example of the ingenuity and humor that he hoped his friend would be remembered for.

The last words that Berkeley wrote, in January 1988, were:

> *Learning to live together is the biggest variable for a computer field's future.*

Reflection

In reflecting upon his legacy for an article published by the IEEE Computer Society History Committee, J. A. N. Lee makes the case that Edmund Berkeley should be considered "the conscience of the computer industry," owing to his long-held conviction that the only legitimate use of computers was for the betterment of humanity, not its destruction.

The struggle between the promise of computing and its destructive potential continued to play out at a global scale in the following decades, both in the real world and in the virtual world. And speculative fiction once again provided a lens for thinking about just what kind of future it would bring.

PART III

Walking Around A Mile High

CHAPTER 7

Walking Around, a Mile High

H.G. Wells summed up the Second Industrial Revolution as having abolished distance. Automobiles and airplanes allowed people to travel more easily and quickly across towns, states, countries, and continents. The speed of travel transformed the experience of distance.

Edmund Berkeley observed emerging computing technology abolishing computation time. Computers could solve equations at superhuman speeds; the speed of their mathematical operations transformed the experience of data.

By the 1980s, data was becoming a commodity. Computers were already widely adopted in industry and government and were beginning to take hold with consumers as well. In the 1990s, computers spanning the globe were connected, and easy access to knowledge about nearly any subject transformed the experience of information.

But the digital transformation of the Information Age was overshadowed by the specter of centralized corporate control of the flow of information. This looming threat sparked fears of a technology-fueled, corporate-sponsored dystopia, and a new generation of writers started exploring these darker, increasingly plausible near-futures.

© Coraline Ada Ehmke 2025
C. A. Ehmke, *We Just Build Hammers*, https://doi.org/10.1007/979-8-8688-1249-1_7

Introducing Neal Stephenson

Author Neal Stephenson was a late-comer to this emerging wave of science fiction, but his contribution to the movement was enormous. His work not only significantly impacted science fiction but inspired an entire generation of technologists.

Born on Halloween in 1959, Stephenson spent his childhood moving between various small cities in the American Midwest, a long series of what he calls MACTs, or "Midwestern American College Towns." He had a comfortable and intellectually stimulating childhood, raised by an engineering professor father and a biochemist mother.

Stephenson was a proud member of the Science Fiction Book Club and describes his childhood as one filled with days of reading. He cites the writer Andre (Alice) Norton as a favorite from that time, particularly enjoying her mixture of science fiction and magic. Her 1968 novel **THE ZERO STONE**, featuring a heroic space-faring gem trader who discovers an ancient artifact belonging to an alien religious cult, was of particular interest to him.

After high school, Stephenson worked for a year as a research assistant at Ames Laboratory in Iowa, a Department of Energy installation that had been the site of uranium preparation during the Manhattan Project. Some of his childhood friends in Ames had fathers who had been involved with the project. He once reflected that World War II was a time of rapid advances in physics, computing, and encryption; he thought of it as a sort of golden age for technological innovation.

He attended Boston University and graduated in 1981 with a degree in geography, a diversion from his intended major, physics, which he took as a minor. Switching majors gave him access to the geography department's computers, which were in less demand than the computer lab of the physics department.

The Hero-Engineer

Many of Stephenson's beloved childhood books, written on the other side of World War II, featured protagonists of the "hero-engineer" archetype.

This archetype depicted leading characters who relied on their scientific knowledge to meet the challenges facing them, using their ingenuity and ability to solve problems rather than their own physical prowess, weaponry, or charm to overcome obstacles.

Stories featuring hero-engineers often involved the main character inventing a device or technology that became central to resolving (or instigating) the conflict of the story. Without their cleverness and scientific expertise, the worlds of these heroes would fall to catastrophe. This sort of optimistic techno-solutionism was the hallmark of the age: after all, a world war of unprecedented scale had been won in large part due to the concerted effort of technologists.

Stephenson had lots of examples of hero-engineers to draw inspiration from in his writing.

Isaac Asimov's "I, Robot" series features a recurring character in Dr. Susan Calvin, a robopsychologist and cybernetic engineer who works for US Robots and Mechanical Men, Inc., the manufacturer of the robotic race in the stories. Dr. Calvin is portrayed as near-emotionless and uses her keen intellect to untangle bugs in their positronic brains.

In 1968, Arthur C Clarke and Stanley Kubrick wrote the screenplay for **2001: A SPACE ODYSSEY**, which also featured a hero-engineer as its protagonist. Dr. Dave Bowman's intellectual capabilities are pitted against his spaceship's near-omnipotent AI, HAL-9000, requiring him to bring all of his problem-solving and technical skills to bear in order to survive.

Stephenson even cited the 1958 Robert Heinlein juvenile fiction **HAVE SPACESUIT, WILL TRAVEL** as a favorite read from his youth. The book tells the story of an ingenious boy named Kip, a young and brilliant engineer, who repairs and restores a secondhand space suit that he won in a contest. While wearing his newly refurbished suit, Kip is abducted by aliens, starting him on a series of adventures spanning the galaxy.

He didn't immediately begin writing speculative fiction. Stephenson published his first novel, an academic comedy titled **The Big** U, in 1984, followed by the eco-thriller **Zodiac** in 1988.

Rise of the Dystopia

A dystopic current had been running through science fiction since the New Wave era of writers in the 1960s, including Philip K Dick, Samuel Delany, and Harlan Ellison. Science fiction had long been a venue for telling stories about our collective hopes for the future. And while moral conundrums were common fare in speculative fiction, even the most grim tales usually had a spark of optimism.

Where dystopian futures were once the *subjects* of cautionary tales, by the 1980s, dystopias became merely the *settings* for such stories, a prefabricated backdrop for tales of bleak tomorrows. Dystopia became the default. This shift marked the birth of the cyberpunk genre.

Techno-dystopias are central to cyberpunk, often portrayed as a world collapsing under the weight of high-tech capitalism.

Cyberpunk flipped the hero-engineer concept of earlier periods of science fiction on its head. The term "cyberpunk," coined by author Bruce Bethke in 1980, was intended to communicate the idea of technological troublemakers. These troublemakers, often dubbed "hackers," were, as author Bruce Sterling described, "high-tech low-lifes," vaguely criminal underdogs who knew how to use technology to subvert the unjust systems that dominated their lives and their worlds.

Unlike the space-faring heroes and alien encounters of earlier ages of science fiction, the antiheroes of cyberpunk lived in worlds representing plausible near-futures, often only a decade or two away. In these futures, the political, economic, and social issues of the day played out to their extremes, under systems of oppression whose reach and impact was magnified by pervasive, almost suffocating tech.

Snow Crash

Snow Crash was written in the years 1988 through 1991 as the author listened to a great deal of loud, relentless, depressing music.

—From "About the Author," **SNOW CRASH**

For Neal Stephenson's third novel, he turned to the gritty, almost noir-like science fiction coming out of the cyberpunk movement. William Gibson's **NEUROMANCER** was his first introduction to the genre and opened up an enticing new world to him. He painted his own picture of this kind of world in what proved to be the most impactful novel of his career to date: 1992's **SNOW CRASH**.

Poised somewhere between a love letter and a satire of the cyberpunk genre, **SNOW CRASH** tells the story of Hiro Protagonist, a pizza delivery driver and hacker who gets tangled up in an epic struggle between the Mafia, a megachurch minister, and a media mogul.

While the author has been quoted as saying that he believed many of the ideas in **SNOW CRASH** were "obvious," the cultural and technological influence of the book can't be understated. The book cemented the word "avatar" in its contemporary meaning as one's digital representation, inspired the creation of Google Earth, and provided a compelling portrayal of the Internet as a three-dimensional virtual world. This concept directly influenced the development of first-person online games like **QUAKE**, the virtual reality environment **SECOND LIFE**, and the massively multiplayer online role-playing games that followed.

Stephenson's work shows a keen awareness of the interconnectedness of technology and society and all the complexity that comes with their intertwining. It's the impact of irrepressible technological progress that interests him.

Life in the Burbclaves

The plot of **SNOW CRASH** moves between two worlds: the physical world, in a perpetual state of social, political, and economic collapse, and an immersive virtual world, the Metaverse.

The "real world" in **SNOW CRASH** is a dismal, decayed projection of our trajectory as a society. The book depicts the remains of America as a nightmarish vision of anarcho-capitalism writ large. People live in private, franchise-owned gated suburbs called Burbclaves, each catering to a particular class of resident. White Columns, for example, provides a comfortable neighborhood for white supremacists and their families.

Those who can't afford a house in a posh Burbclave take shelter wherever they can, like the hero of the novel, who lives with a roommate in a shipping container.

The vestiges of government have been absorbed into corporations like the Central Intelligence Corporation, a privatized mash-up of the CIA and the Library of Congress. Everything that can possibly be privatized has been privatized.

Even street gangs have gone corporate: the American Mafia owns franchise locations in all the worst neighborhoods of Los Angeles. And the sky is filled with an inescapable haze of advertisements and billboards and signs, the "loglo."

The Metaverse

The dimensions of the Street are fixed by a protocol, hammered out by the computer-graphics ninja overlords of the Association for Computing Machinery's Global Multimedia Protocol Group.

—Neal Stephenson, **SNOW CRASH**

Stephenson's Metaverse is a welcome escape from the capitalist decay of the real world. Immersed in the virtual world, people navigate their three-dimensional avatars among markets, clubs, concert halls, and other digital real estate lining a 65,536-kilometer-long road bisecting a 10,000-kilometer-diameter black sphere hanging in empty space.

Free rapid transit via monorail connects 256 stations, or ports, spaced evenly along the Street, many of which are surrounded by digital development. People also use these stations as an unobtrusive way of entering and exiting the Metaverse. Simply appearing or disappearing in space would be visually jarring and socially rude.

Hiro Protagonist, as a long-term resident of the Metaverse, has a stake in the Black Sun, an exclusive virtual club that's home to contingents of both hackers and rock stars. It's his headquarters, his hideout, and the place where he feels he belongs. It's different in every way from the mad world outside his shipping container home.

Building Blocks of Code

Every structure and object in the Metaverse is built of code, and every interaction is subject to a small number of fundamental rules, a set of digital laws of nature. It's an irrational sort of world but within rational bounds.

The Metaverse's foundation of logic and binary numbers had an almost mystical appeal to the hacker mind. There are repeating manifestations of the powers of 2, like the 2^{16} length of the Street. There are some numbers like these that Stephenson describes as more recognizable to a hacker than the date of their own mother's birthday.

Stephenson even imagines a role for the Association of Computing Machinery, Berkeley's ACM, in the design of the Metaverse. A special interest group called the Global Multimedia Protocol Group was responsible for the fundamental design constraints and establishing the protocols by which the objects, places, and people rendered in code could interact with each other and the environment.

Social norms reflect a power hierarchy tilted in favor of the hacker. Virtual real estate is available for purchase, but you need to know how to code if you want to build something there. Goods that can be exchanged are also just programs under the surface. Information is quite literally the fundamental building block of this reality.

Each person in the Metaverse is represented by their own personal avatar. An avatar can be pretty much anything that a citizen of the Metaverse wants, but no matter the shape, it can't be taller than the real-world person, to "prevent people from walking around a mile high": socially disruptive, an obvious prank, and a serious distraction from the serious business of the Metaverse.

People invest heavily in their avatars, which also serve as signifiers of social status. Those who enter the Metaverse from public terminals are called black-and-whites, owing to the low-resolution, desaturated default avatars of anonymous users.

Normative standards overlap between the real and virtual worlds, but the extrinsic forces that shape or manipulate them were different. The external world is beholden to the analog irrationality of capitalism, the internal world to the digital tyranny of binaries.

Technical, normative, and social standards help keep the peace between the estimated 60 million simultaneous occupants of the Metaverse. The virtual world could be a dangerous, unpredictable place, but it is still a welcome respite from the grinding dystopia of the outside world.

The Bicameral Mind

Enki had the ability to ascend into the universe of language and see it before his eyes. Much as humans go into the Metaverse.

—Neal Stephenson, **Snow Crash**

The name of the novel refers to a hybrid digital/biological virus called "Snow Crash," which could be transmitted into a hacker's brain visually via a specially encoded bitmap image of static (snow). The victims of the virus faced a future with both their computers and their brains reduced to useless junk.

The concept of a mind virus that can be transmitted by information is likely inspired by the then-nascent practice of neurolinguistic programming, which posits that the human mind can be programmed (or reprogrammed) by deliberately manipulating the connections between language, behavior, and neurological systems. It also brings to mind science fiction veteran Samuel Delany's 1966 **Babel**-17, which features a language that can act as a weapon.

In an interview with journalist James Mustich, Stephenson acknowledged that a book by consciousness researcher Julian Jaynes, titled **The Origin of Consciousness in the Breakdown of the Bicameral Mind**, was also a significant influence on **Snow Crash**.

Jaynes's theory of the bicameral mind posits that consciousness as we know it first emerged in humans around 2000 BCE, among the people of Greece and Mesopotamia. It emerged when humans learned to internalize the voice of conscience and will, uniting the two chambers of their brains. Prior to this mental unification, messages from the separated hemisphere were passed to the individual through auditory hallucinations of the voices of gods, spirits, ancestors, and demons.

In Stephenson's tale, the businessman extraordinaire L. Bob Rife, whose headquarters is a decommissioned aircraft carrier, is involved in a plot with the larger-than-life Reverend Wayne, of Reverend Wayne's Pearly Gates, Inc. Rife plans to use the Snow Crash mind virus to infect the population and make them susceptible to his manipulation. Essentially, he's scheming to return humanity to the bicameral state that Jaynes described, using his virtual voice of god to direct the thoughts and lives of his helpless followers.

Giving in to this mental manipulation means giving up responsibility for your own actions; reverting to the bicameral mind takes the pressure of decision-making away, as everything you do is literally following orders. This dismal state almost has an appeal in a world where individual decisions and the exercise of free will are already so meaningless in the face of widespread chaos and perpetual catastrophe.

At a key point in the story, inspiration for an antidote to the digital virus comes from the Mesopotamian myth of Enki. According to ancient legend, Enki had invented a prayer or spell, the *nam-shub*, that freed the people of Sumeria from the linguistic mind control of the priesthood by making the Sumerian language incomprehensible to them. (Many scholars believe that the story of Enki's *nam-shub* provided the inspiration for the myth of the Tower of Babel.)

The cure to Snow Crash involved mixing in a small program that Hiro wrote, called SnowScan. SnowScan could block the conscience-numbing effect of the virus and maintain the would-be victim's full sentience. Like Wells and Berkeley before him, Stephenson makes a case for rationality, logic, and reason to return the mad world to some semblance of sanity and security.

Power Disorders

Stephenson clearly has opinions about the future of unmitigated capitalism and the collapse of the economic and political foundations of the United States. But in interviews and essays, Stephenson remains reticent about his specific political views.

However, an interview with Mike Godwin for **REASON** magazine in 2005 revealed at least some of Stephenson's political leanings. While noting that he had libertarians among his fans and acknowledging that almost any sort of interaction with the government acts as a "recruiting station" for libertarians, he sees a dangerous possibility of a stable system developing around self-perpetuating conflict between statists, libertarians, and terrorists.

In the interview, Stephenson quoted a theologian named Walter Wink and described how, in the face of inscrutable systems of domination, we learn certain tricks for survival but can fail to perceive how the larger system actually works.

The situation is likened to the times before germ theory, where the causes of disease were not understood but there were certain things that could be done—like boarding up a house stricken by the plague—that seemed to keep it from spreading.

In an interview about his book **TERMINATION SHOCK** in 2021, Stephenson pointed to social media sites, and the corporations running them, as a source of "highly optimized disinformation" that, incredibly, was able to convince a large number of people during the first waves of the COVID epidemic that the disease was not even real. He observed that if it's that difficult to convince people that hundreds of thousands of people are "drop[ping] dead all around them," it's going to be nearly impossible to convey the criticality of dealing with something as "far away" as the climate crisis. It seems that nothing can stand in the way of the profit-seeking corporations that have amassed such power over what people consider real or unreal.

Stephenson calls unjust disparities in power a "power disorder" and sees a role for both legal and social recourse in dealing with them. Speaking of Wink, he says, "he is clearly all in favor of people standing up against oppressive power systems of all stripes." This is a consistent theme in Stephenson's fiction.

In an essay titled "It's All Geek to Me," Stephenson criticizes conservatives who have "cut all ties to their own intellectual moorings" and notes that the only conservatives who remain committed to science are the libertarians. "As far as geeks are concerned," he writes, "I think they're all just stunned and aghast at the turn that politics has taken in my country towards a frank disregard of scientific reality."

Despite his distrust of concentrations of power, his critique of libertarianism, and his cautionary tales of capitalism run amuck, a number of billionaires count themselves among Stephenson's fans. One critic, noting the attention given to Stephenson by the likes of Bill Gates, Sergey Brin, and Jeff Bezos, referred to him as the "Billionaire's Bard."

Future Tense

In a 2011 article titled "Innovation Starvation," published in the journal of the World Policy Institute, Stephenson recalled the story of an experience he had at a conference called Future Tense earlier that year. One of the other speakers at the conference, Arizona State University president Michael Crow, accused contemporary science fiction writers of "slacking off." Stephenson took this to mean that the scientists and engineers of the world are waiting for science fiction to tell them what to work on next. Essentially, the speaker was saying that it is the responsibility of writers to supply the "big visions" that will lead to major technological breakthroughs.

In his 1998 book **ACHIEVING OUR COUNTRY**, philosopher Richard Rorty cites **SNOW CRASH** as an example of a wave of a hopeless sort of literature poisoning American culture. Rorty critiques the novel as depicting a world where knowledge is valued more than hope, and warns that its impact on the psyche of modern Americans could become a self-fulfilling prophecy.

Regardless of whether or not Stephenson actually took criticism like this to heart, much of his subsequent work, even when still dark and technological, is less hopeless. While continuing to write cautionary tales of the near future, his settings put distance between his stories and the overtly dystopian worlds still so prevalent in other works of speculative fiction.

Project Hieroglyph

Further evidence that Stephenson grew dissatisfied with dystopia came in direct response to the Arizona State University president's callout. In April of 2013, the University's Center for Science and the Imagination launched Project Hieroglyph as a collaborative effort between the school and Neal Stephenson.

The project's goal was to connect writers of speculative fiction with researchers, students, and scientists to create next-generation science fiction that was something of a return to the techno-optimism of previous eras of the genre.

In describing the origin of the name, Stephenson related an exchange he had with a researcher at Microsoft. Over the course of the conversation with Jim Karkanias, the term "hieroglyph" came up as a sort of shorthand for iconic, immediately recognizable concepts in science fiction. What was needed, they decided, was a new set of hieroglyphs, a new set of iconic concepts to guide the thinking and dreaming of new generations of scientists and engineers worldwide.

In a university press release, the director of the Center suggested that what science fiction does best is to not just provide the idea for a new technology but to show how it might integrate into people's lives. This brings to mind the principle behind Wells's Law: the domestication of a future technology in a techno-social context.

As Stephenson said in a 2008 **DER SPIEGEL** interview, "Books can be useful as a rallying point for people to organize their thinking."

A 20 Kilometer Tower

The work done under the auspices of Project Hieroglyph was not purely literary. The unique pairing of writers with engineers allowed both kinds of practitioners to bring their skills to bear in imagining future innovations.

As part of the project, science fiction writer Cory Doctorow was paired with Kip Hodges, director of the School of Earth and Space Exploration at Arizona State University, to consider whether 3D-printed structures built from lunar dust might make human habitation on the moon a possibility.

A collaboration between Neal Stephenson and Keith Hjelmstad, Professor of Structural Engineering at ASU, explored the question of building a steel tower that was 20 kilometers high: high enough to extend into the very upper reaches of the atmosphere and even to see the curvature of the earth. The project attracted the interest of other collaborators, including architects and aerospace engineers. Beyond being an engineering marvel for the centuries, such a tower could make a huge impact in the delivery of payloads into space.

Director Hjelmstad was quoted saying that the fundamental question behind the tower concept ("how tall can humans build something?") is the kind of question that immediately sparks curiosity and enthusiasm, tapping into the passion and ambition of engineers and students alike.

Is It Too Late for Techno-optimism?

Project Hieroglyph published an anthology of some of its engineer-writer collaborations in 2014, titled **Hieroglyph: Stories & Visions for a Better Future**. The anthology featured work by Elizabeth Bear, Cory Doctorow, Karl Schroeder, and Bruce Sterling, among others. The book is a treasure trove of techno-optimism, exploring topics including sustainable energy, privacy, security, and immigration.

The only constraint placed on contributors to the collection was that there should be no mention of "hackers, hyperspace, or holocaust."

One of the stories, titled "By the Time We Get to Arizona" and written by Madeline Ashby, imagines an immigration policy involving "auditioning" for the role of a visa-holding immigrant. Applicants are invited to live for six weeks in a border town named Mariposa, where their behavior is subject to constant monitoring and surveillance. As the would-be immigrants go about their daily lives, at work, at play, doing the shopping, and a thousand other mundane tasks in the city, the residents are continually upvoting or downvoting each individual or family that participated in the trial period. Those who accumulate the most social capital are be granted visas. While the concept may seem grim, the story follows a particular couple, Ulicez and Alina, who navigate the complexity of the program with love and humor, showing the resilience of humanity in the face of pervasive (and invasive) technology. In a note to the story, the author emphasized the central idea of citizenship as performance and stated her intention for the story to raise fundamental questions about the future of international borders.

The Hieroglyph anthology received the "Most Significant Futures Work" award issued by the Association of Professional Futurists in 2015. In 2016, Project Hieroglyph published a second anthology, titled Slow Catastrophes, Uncertain Revivals, featuring research-based, student-created fiction, to wide critical acclaim.

Present Tense

Stephenson is often critical of the state of technology in the first decades of the twenty-first century. He's written about how short-sightedness is incentivized by our current economic system, meaning that it's increasingly difficult to pursue anything that requires time or risk.

He attributes this rising risk-aversion, ironically, to technology itself. A near-instant web search makes every novel idea turn out to be either something that someone has already tried and failed at or something that someone else has already succeeded with.

Stephenson sees the contemporary regulatory environment as being out of step with the current state of technology, systems of rules so attuned to old ways of doing things that they present barriers to progress. He's particularly outspoken about regulations on nuclear energy, claiming that lack of investment in nuclear energy research has prevented serious progress being made in divesting our energy economy of dependence on oil.

When asked by **REASON** magazine's Mike Godwin if the United States was experiencing a burst of progress, he replied that serious science "isn't really being fostered by mainstream culture" anymore. He's repeatedly talked about how today's technologists are not taking risks and have become incapable of "executing the big stuff." He also noted the growing trend of an antiscience stance among the American political right, which he perceives as another threat to public support of technological progress.

But where government and private sector innovation are failing in his eyes, pockets of revolutionary, decentralized technologists provide him with a spark of hope. In a 2004 interview in **THE GUARDIAN**, Stephenson spoke enthusiastically about open source software. Like the hi-tech underdogs of cyberpunk, he sees open source developers being in a position to leverage their knowledge of systems to subvert the dominant corporate culture of the modern world.

Unlike the lone underdogs of fiction, however, Stephenson believes that interpersonal cohesion is a hard requirement for today's hackers. In the same **GUARDIAN** article, he praised open source it for being a global, "collective enterprise" in which "solitary geniuses need not apply." Stephenson held up open source software as proof that, for a better technological future, "social and organizational skills are of the essence."

In a conversation with **VANITY FAIR** reporter Joanna Robinson, Stephenson was asked how different the Metaverse would be if it was controlled by a large corporation like Facebook. He responded by saying that with every invention, it's not always possible to predict the impact or results.

"At some level," he said, "it boils down to people's capacity to act as socially responsible, ethical individuals."

Reflection

The heroes of cyberpunk were scrappy hackers who knew how to use (and abuse) technology to save the world. But while the protagonists of this new form of speculative fiction tended to be lone actors, writers like Neal Stephenson believed that without a strong sense of connection to our communities and to society as a whole, there would be no way for anyone to stave off dystopia.

As the possibility of an oppressive technology-fueled future seemed to grow closer every day, a new generation of technologists would have to take up the challenge of ensuring that computers were a force for good.

CHAPTER 8

The Ego and the id

In defining the constraints around the techno-optimistic **Hieroglyph** anthology, Neal Stephenson had forbidden the appearance of hackers altogether. This wasn't because he had lost respect for hackers, but because he wanted to challenge the compelling fantasy of a lone hacker saving the world. As he expressed in his assessment of open source, he believed that the technological solutions the world needed most were going to come from socially cohesive, collective effort.

In Stephenson's depiction of the capitalist dystopia that forms the backdrop for **Snow Crash**, the decentralized nature of the Metaverse makes it one of the few areas of modern life that was able to resist corporate control. Even though corporations had a presence there, some even building virtual headquarters along the Street, the Metaverse was firmly under the control of the technologically savvy, acting within the constraints set up by the ACM.

In the real world, corporate capture was not so easily resisted. As computers were increasingly adopted by business, the software that those businesses relied upon became commercialized. Once computer scientists enjoyed a collegial sort of fellowship across institutional borders. Now, computer corporations were closing the doors on the production of software. As the personal computer was commoditized, so was the software that ran on it.

© Coraline Ada Ehmke 2025
C. A. Ehmke, *We Just Build Hammers*, https://doi.org/10.1007/979-8-8688-1249-1_8

Cyberpunk worlds like that of **Snow Crash** operate solely on the basis of controlling the flow of information, with agents on decentralized networks competing against those from global megacorporations. All of this seemed to come under threat as computers became more and more a part of daily life.

The cyberpunk genre reinforced many of the long-standing values and beliefs held by computer technologists. The early hacker movement of the 1970s espoused the free flow of information, a distrust of centralized systems of any kind, and a playful sort of technical mastery.

Hackers in cyberpunk stories have enviable technical expertise, but survive or thrive through their cleverness and unpredictability. And throughout all their adventures and misadventures, there is a complex and subtle ethical code in play, just below the surface.

This code has been described as the hacker ethic.

The Hacker Ethic

In his 1984 book **Hackers: Heroes of the Computer Revolution**, journalist Steven Levy presented a compelling study of hacker culture. He traces the origins of some of the fundamental beliefs of the hacker community and explores how they manifest over time.

The history of this fascinating subculture is told through personal stories of key figures in computing, some well-known and some lesser-known, from the 1960s and 1970s.

Levy describes the hacker ethic as having its roots in a tight-knit community of technologists, computer scientists, and computer enthusiasts at MIT. The story begins with the Tech Model Railroad Club splintering into two factions, one obsessed with the trains and landscapes and the other with the complex wiring and components that powered the dioramas.

Later, the Artificial Intelligence Lab became a magnet for hackers of all stripes, and in Levy's interviews, several people remarked on the fact that one could simply show up at any time of night and find at least a few hackers clustered around a computer, engrossed in solving some arcane problem or another. The tales from this era describe a madcap mix of petty larceny, elaborate pranks, and epic hacks.

Eventually, of course, the culture moved on, leaving behind a small nostalgic contingent to witness the rise of new generations of hackers.

Levy's book draws attention to the social and cultural norms that arose from the early hacker community and that have persisted across successive generations. Levy presents six key tenets or virtues that he understands to be the near-universal, fundamental ethos of the hacker archetype: the "hands-on" imperative, freedom of information, distrust of authority, meritocracy, beauty in code, and the life-changing potential of computers.

The Hands-On Imperative

When you first turn on a computer, it is an inert collection of circuits that can't really do anything. To start up the machine, you have to infuse those circuits with a collection of rules that tell it how to function. How to be a computer.

—Neil Stephenson, **Snow Crash**

The "Hands-On Imperative" is perhaps the most fundamental precept of the hacker ethic. It's about universal access to systems. Everyone should have the right to take something apart to understand how it works; even better, there's an expectation that they will improve upon it for the greater good.

Getting hands-on with a technology sometimes involves reverse-engineering, deducing how a system works by observing how it behaves. Sometimes free access to resources, whether physical, like a terminal, or virtual, like a database, requires ignoring certain rules and regulations around privacy, security, and intellectual property.

As the action in **Snow Crash** comes to a crescendo, Hiro's uncanny ability to reverse-engineer software is the only thing that prevents the neurolinguistic virus from infecting a quarter of a million hackers in the Metaverse. His deep understanding of the underlying protocols allows him to hack its "reality" itself. For example, Hiro sometimes takes advantage of laggy satellite network connections to pass through solid walls, and he programmed a virtual katana capable of causing damage to avatars.

The Hands-On Imperative has given rise to several antiproprietary movements, including most recently the Right to Repair movement, which seeks to guarantee that the owner of a piece of technology, whether a cell phone or an automobile or a piece of farm equipment, can maintain and modify the machine without the manufacturer's permission or interference.

Decentralized Everything

Besides, interesting things happen along borders—transitions—not in the middle where everything is the same.

—Neil Stephenson, **Snow Crash**

Levy hones in on another fundamental principle in identifying decentralization as having a particular appeal to the hacker. Centralized control goes against the right to access anything from anywhere. Bureaucracy, whether corporate, governmental, or academic, introduces barriers that tilted power to their advantage, recalling Stephenson's "power disorders."

Cyberpunk often depicts decentralized systems defeating centralized systems. In **Snow Crash**, the chaotic, distributed Metaverse was the only place where Hiro could circumvent the hypercorporate powers-that-be. Owing to its lack of central control, Hiro was able to move, interact, hack, and trespass in ways that would have been difficult or impossible given the regulations and realities of the physical world.

The globally distributed Metaverse also served as a place for like-minded individuals to come together despite geographical boundaries, just as the early Internet made possible. Hiro was able to make allies and friends from around the world, without whom the world would have been wracked by a digital apocalypse.

Beautiful Code

Well, all information looks like noise until you break the code.

—Neal Stephenson, **Snow Crash**

Steven Levy noted that computer hackers dealt with significant constraints on the size of the programs that early computers could manage. This led to the practice of "bumming," akin to what today is sometimes called "code golf," a sort of intellectual game of refactoring a piece of code to its smallest possible size.

Stephenson's book spends a great deal of time on the almost numerological binary obsessions of the architects of the Metaverse specifications. Hiro has an obvious respect for the directness and simplicity of its underlying protocols, on top of which so much complexity could be built and flourish.

While most contemporary software developers enjoy the freedom of using high-level languages and don't have to be quite so terse with their code as in decades before, we are still captive to the idea of beauty expressed in code. A component or even an entire system may be recognized as "elegant," appealing to a sort of intellectual aesthetic sensibility that developers may find difficult to articulate but easy to identify.

Meritocracy

Class is more than income, it has to do with knowing where you stand in a web of social relationships.

—Neal Stephenson, **Snow Crash**

Levy observed that hackers tended to organize themselves socially into a sort of hierarchy governed by one's perceived technical capabilities. Competition for social capital took the form of seeking ever more elegant hacks, with the value of contributions to the body of computing knowledge being the measure of personal worth within the hacker community.

This techno-social currency model is essentially meritocratic in nature. As such, it mirrors a hacker virtue that Levy articulated as hackers being judged by their hacking, rather than "bogus criteria such as degrees, age, race, or position."

Meritocracy seemed to offer a solution to the problem of power disparities between computer programmers and their employers or institutions. Traditional measures of authority were mocked and undermined, with managers and other nontechnical types deemed unworthy of much attention.

Hackers were reacting to the same kind of social issues that are parodied in the physical world of **Snow Crash**, with hierarchies of authority built on greed, violence, and mountains of capital. But in the Metaverse, authority came from the social currency of one's perceived technical capabilities. It was there that hackers were valued for their skills and ingenuity and rewarded with access and fame. This was the organizing principle behind meritocracy.

Meritocracy is fundamentally a utilitarian form of social governance. The system rewards participants who contribute the most. The unit of value produced by the hacker meritocracy is knowledge or information.

On its surface, meritocracy appears to be a rational system that provides a simple and elegant solution to problems of inclusion and exclusion, belonging and othering, and this appeals to the age-old desire of technologists for society to adhere to rational principles. It is a return to the bicameral mind, with the voice of reason taking the place of the voice of gods in directing one's moral actions.

Computers Are Life-Changing

So the hacker perspective isn't just the point of view of a few geeks. It is everyone's perspective now.

—Neal Stephenson, quoted in *The Guardian*,
November 2004

Levy identified the transformative nature of a close, even symbiotic relationship between a hacker and a computer as essential to the hacker ethos.

One thing that technologists from the days of Berkeley and the UNIVAC and the technologists of the modern Internet age can agree on is the life-changing nature of our relationships to computers. Without his sleek computer rig, Hiro would have been just another sword-wielding pizza delivery driver.

The development of communities of hackers, either in-person or virtual, created opportunities for connections and the exchange of knowledge that would otherwise be out of reach.

Berkeley wanted a world where computer technology was accessible and understandable to everyone, not just highly skilled IBM engineers or computer scientists in university labs. In this spirit, hackers at MIT's Artificial Intelligence Lab secretly allowed local technically inclined teenagers to sneak in and use the lab's computers for free.

Fortunes and futures were made possible by intrepid hackers pushing the boundaries of what computers were capable of and who could have access to them.

Source Code Is Free Speech

The Metaverse is a fictional structure made out of code. And code is just a form of speech—the form that computers understand.

—Neil Stephenson, **SNOW CRASH**

The last of the six hacker virtues that Levy writes about is the belief in the free flow of information. Information is defined as anything that can be represented with ones and zeroes, including software.

In the early days of punch card programming, computer scientists would put aside specially labeled cards that made a given task a little easier; this was the beginning of the "tools to make tools" movement in software development.

With information and code moving freely within a community, improvements can be made to the benefit of everyone. Duplicated effort can be avoided. New efficiencies can be gained.

H.G. Wells imagined a world brain that contained the sum of human knowledge, and cyberpunk depictions of the Internet are clear examples of the concept. **SNOW CRASH** has Hiro exploring a database of Sumerian history and mythology with the help of a literal-minded Librarian daemon. Today, this virtue of open and free information is manifest in things like Wikipedia—and, of course, free and open source software, often abbreviated as FOSS.

The Four Freedoms

They made data a controlled substance.

—Neal Stephenson, **Snow Crash**

Proprietary software had been bumping up against the hacker ethic since the late 1970s. At MIT's Artificial Intelligence Lab in 1983, the pressure was rising.

The infamous lab was tucked in at Tech Square in Cambridge, Massachusetts. Tech Square was adjacent to the MIT campus and comprised a city block featuring a squat, square building in the center surrounded on three sides by taller office buildings. Much of the original hacker culture that Steven Levy wrote about had originated there, and the lab was in many ways a microcosm of what was happening in the broader computing world.

As students and engineers at the lab saw opportunities to turn their passions into businesses, leaving behind their tight-knit community of hackers at MIT, some of those who stayed behind felt a sense of abandonment, like their culture was being eroded by the forces of capitalism.

Among them was Richard Stallman, who worked as a programmer and research assistant at the lab. In a speech given at New York University in May 2001, Stallman told the story of a Xerox laser printer that had been gifted to MIT and networked with the lab's computers. He described the printer as a glorified office copier. The machine frequently jammed, and there was no way for a user to know that the 20-minute print job they had started ended with a paper jam after printing only a few pages.

Stallman wanted to do what any programmer at the time would want to do: to improve the printer driver software so that it reported back errors to the user. But the Xerox printer software did not ship with source code, and in fact, Xerox felt no particular obligation to make it available.

Stallman considered access to source code, and the ability to modify and improve it, as a fundamental freedom that should be afforded to all computer users. He could see the world shifting away from this perspective and undertook a lifelong campaign to push back against its inevitability.

From the GNU Project, an initiative to write a free-software-powered, UNIX-like operating system, to GNU Emacs, a version of the popular text editor distributed with the condition that improvements be given back, Stallman began to distill a set of three (eventually, four) essential "freedoms" that he believed were fundamental human rights. (He has referred to "non-free software" as "a crime against humanity.")

The Four Freedoms, as they would come to be known, specified the conditions under which software could be considered conforming to his ideals of freedom: the source code of the software must be inspectable and changeable, copyable, and distributable, and modified or extended versions of the software must be allowed to be made available. But the primary condition, Freedom Zero, insisted that the software be free to use for any purpose, without any restriction.

These Four Freedoms were intended as an ethical framework specific to the world of computing. They were soon encoded into a new software license, the GNU Public License (GPL), and promoted by Stallman's new nonprofit, the Free Software Foundation.

Talk Is Cheap, Show Me the Code

When Hiro learned how to do this, way back fifteen years ago, a hacker could sit down and write an entire piece of software by himself. Now, that's no longer possible.

—Neil Stephenson, **Snow Crash**

The influence of the Free Software philosophy was soon felt around the world, and the GNU Public License gained traction. The elegant hack of invoking intellectual property rights to protect free access to code was paying off.

A striking example of the success of the free software ethos could be found in Helsinki, Finland, with a Swedish-speaking computer programmer named Linus Torvalds.

In a 2008 interview with Grady Booch, Torvalds recalled learning English in his preteen years by reading science fiction. English-language books and magazines were cheaper than their Finnish counterparts. He told Booch that he preferred the "hard science" of Isaac Asimov and Robert Heinlein, citing **STRANGER IN A STRANGE LAND** as a particular favorite.

Torvalds was using Stallman's GNU tools to develop his own operating system kernel, dubbed F-R-E-A-X (later, thankfully, renamed to Linux). He had worked on Linux since 1991, at first as "just a hobby," soon as an obsession, and eventually as a lucrative career.

An early version of Linux was released under a license restricting commercial use. But version 0.12 was relicensed under the GPL. This change in mindset, adopting a license that permitted free use by anyone, was likely inspired after Torvalds saw Stallman speak at a nearby university. The notion of fighting for technological freedom likely appealed to the young programmer, recalling the scientific heroism of his early reading.

Linux came along at just the right time. The hobby operating system provided an increasingly compelling alternative to the market dominance of Microsoft Windows. Microsoft soon recognized Linux as an existential threat. A collection of internal memos, the so-called "Halloween Documents," was leaked in October of 1998 and detailed Microsoft's secret strategy to discredit Linux in favor of its own operating system. The memos described an organized campaign to spread what hackers called FUD (fear, uncertainty, and doubt) about the danger and irresponsibility of adopting FOSS.

Today, Linux is considered one of the most successful FOSS projects in history and is widely considered the premiere operating system for Internet servers, mobile devices, and scientific computing applications.

The Doom That Came to Linux

Making Snow Crash into a reality feels like a sort of moral imperative to a lot of programmers.

—John Carmack

While some programmers, like Linus Torvalds, were attracted to the ideology of free software, other prominent developers seemed to wander into FOSS almost by accident.

Michael Abrash was well-known in computer game development circles for his groundbreaking book on graphics programming. While he was still employed at Microsoft, working on Windows NT, he was approached by a young man named John Carmack, founder of id Software and creator of a game called **Doom**.

Doom had made a huge impact on the computer gaming world, and by 1995, it was installed on more computers than Windows 95 itself. (**Doom** was also the first id title ported to Linux, in 1994.) So Abrash was intrigued by Carmack's suggestion that they collaborate on a new game.

Over the course of their meeting, Stephenson's **Snow Crash** came up as a point of mutual interest. Quoted in the book **Masters of Doom**, Abrash recalls thinking of the Metaverse and realizing that he knew how to do about 80% of it himself and that he had no doubt that he was "sitting across from a twenty-four-year-old who had the skills and confidence to make [the rest of it] happen."

Abrash left Microsoft to work with Carmack at id in 1995. id was headquartered at Town East Tower in Mesquite, Texas. Dubbed "The Black Cube," it was a featureless black-glass building that brings to mind Stephenson's featureless Black Sun club in the Metaverse. It was there that the pair led the development of id's new blockbuster game, **Quake**.

With multiplayer support and radically advanced 3D rendering, **Quake** was the closest thing to the Metaverse that had come out of computing. When the game was released in 1996, it was clear that Abrash and Carmack's collaboration had created a worthy successor to the groundbreaking **Doom**. They had also significantly advanced the state of the art in game development and computer graphics.

Carmack had insisted since the early days of id that the games they produced should be easy for users to modify. A whole modding subculture had grown around **Doom** and **Quake**, and Carmack saw this as a way of extending the lifespan of a given game. If fans of the game continued making new content and adding new features, people would be motivated to keep playing.

In the spirit of promoting community involvement in the game, Carmack made the case for releasing the source code for **Doom** under a noncommercial license on December 23, 1997. The "DOOM Source Code License" specified that the source code could only be used for educational purposes, could not be used for commercial purposes, and was not free to redistribute.

In 1999, riding the rising wave of free software, **Doom** was relicensed under Stallman's GNU GPL. id adopted the practice of releasing the source code for the prior game whenever a new game in the **Quake** series was launched.

All Bugs Are Shallow

Ideology is a virus.

—Neal Stephenson, **Snow Crash**

Even as the Free Software movement was gaining momentum, there were some hackers who felt that its almost militant ideological underpinnings would make the model unpalatable to businesses, which would bring about the downfall of the movement just when it was needed most.

In 1997, a computer programmer named Eric S Raymond published an essay titled "The Cathedral and the Bazaar." In the essay, Raymond described two models of software development: the Cathedral model and the Bazaar model.

In the Cathedral model, the code is written in sequestered chambers by an elite few; although the source code is provided with each release, the decisions and effort put into the release were opaque. There was no record of who made what change and why.

Raymond proposed an alternative method of software development, in which code was written collaboratively and in public. As it turns out, Raymond had learned of this style of community-driven development by observing the behavior of contributors to the Linux kernel.

The fact that the essay was written as a direct critique of the software development approach used by Richard Stallman was no secret: Raymond even cited Stallman's GNU Emacs and GCC as singular examples of the flawed Cathedral model.

In a June 2012 blog post, Raymond repeatedly referred to Stallman as a fanatic, criticizing his ideology and idealism as detrimental to the success of free and open source software.

The Hackers vs. Microsoft

The free exchange of software was one of the hallmarks of early hobbyist computing. In fact, most computer magazines in the 1970s and 1980s contained source code listings for games and other software that could be carefully typed directly into the reader's computer.

The commercialization of software for microcomputers came as something of a culture shock. The most easily cited example is that of Altair BASIC, an interpreter that allowed a user to program their computer using the BASIC language. Micro-Soft [sic] sold copies of their interpreter through a deal with the company that manufactured the Altair computer. When Micro-Soft cofounder Bill Gates learned about computer clubs distributing copies of the software he was trying to sell, he wrote an impassioned editorial likening copying software to copying music or books—that is, he framed sharing software as theft.

The conflict between the "open" and "closed" software worlds would soon escalate to an all-out war.

While Linux threatened Microsoft's proprietary Windows operating systems, the war for the soul of programming was soon fought on a new front as well. By 1995, the Internet had gained popular attention and there was intense competition to build browsers for the nascent World Wide Web. The Web brought individuals, communities, and corporations together in a shared virtual space: a primitive sort of Metaverse. The browser was how you navigated this new world.

While most browsers were freely available for personal use, commercial use required a license. Microsoft made the calculated move of distributing its own browser, Internet Explorer, bundled with its new Windows 95 operating system. For many nontechnical users, there was no distinction between Windows, the Internet, and the browser—everything was available by clicking the Internet Explorer icon.

Microsoft's primary competitor in the so-called Browser Wars was Netscape, whose Navigator browser enjoyed a 72% market share in 1997. But the killer combination of a web browser integrated with an operating system eventually allowed Microsoft to claim nearly 96% market share by 2001.

Netscape, its browser-based business model failing, made the radical decision to release the source code for the browser and gifted it to the newly minted nonprofit Mozilla Foundation for continued development as Mozilla Firefox.

Later, Raymond's "The Cathedral and the Bazaar" would be cited by a former Netscape executive as a factor in their decision. The move to make the source code for their browser free to use, modify, and distribute likely saved the open web.

Defining Open Source

But if life were a mellow elementary school run by well-meaning education Ph.D.s, the Deliverator's report card would say: "Hiro is so bright and creative but needs to work harder on his cooperation skills.

—Neil Stephenson, **Snow Crash**

Netscape's actions made waves throughout the tech community. Sensing that the moment might be right to make a business case, rather than an ideological one, for free software, Eric S Raymond and a small group of technologists gathered in Palo Alto, California, to strategize about a way to leverage the Netscape announcement and make a breakthrough.

The group decided to call their new form of free software "open source" after a suggestion by Christine Peterson.

The choice to be pragmatic in their approach was a deliberate one. Raymond had insisted that moral arguments for free software would alienate businesses and that they should focus on business advantages of open source software, like efficiencies of scale and reduced labor costs for adopters.

Bruce Perens had penned a document the year before, called the "Debian Free Software Guidelines." It outlined the criteria by which the Debian community would decide if a given piece of software was free software or not. The core "open source" group decided to adopt these criteria nearly word for word (while editing out references to Debian) as the official "Open Source Definition."

The Open Source Definition embodied both Stallman's ethical foundation of the Four Freedoms and the build-it-in-the-open approach espoused by Raymond's essay.

Raymond and Perens founded the Open Source Initiative in 1998 to promote the acceptance and adoption of open source software, a practical (and hopefully more palatable to the business world) iteration of free software. The Open Source Definition has remained largely unchanged since then.

Reflection

Berkeley worked hard throughout his career to make computers accessible and comprehensible to everyone. He feared a future where computers were treated as "black boxes," whose operations were as inscrutable as they were critical to the operation of society.

The FOSS movement hearkened back to that aspect of Berkeley's philosophy, by promoting the open discussion, understanding, and sharing of advancements in computing, for the benefit of all. The sharing of helpful code by way of baskets of reusable punch cards had been replaced by FTP servers and CD-ROMs.

By the turn of the twenty-first century, hackers had overcome numerous challenges and won several significant victories, and there was once again hope for an open web. The cyberpunk strategy of using decentralized means to overcome centralized power was playing out in real time on the Internet.

Was the vision of the future that Berkeley promoted being realized? Had the warnings of the cyberpunk authors been heeded? Was a technological dystopia averted? Had the world been saved from corporate control?

Had the hacker ethic really prevailed, or were there fundamental flaws in its foundations that had yet to surface?

CHAPTER 9

We're Building the Torment Nexus

By the early 2000s, the hacker ethic as it was widely understood only reflected half of Edmund Berkeley's vision for the future of computers: open and ubiquitous access. But Berkeley spent his life campaigning for those who build and program computers to accept their larger-than-average share of responsibility to our broader society. He saw this as a necessary counterbalance given the impact of their special skills.

Instead, modern-day FOSS hackers embraced an ethical framework based on unrestricted freedom divorced from accountability. This moral indifference toward broader outcomes and social impact doesn't meet Berkeley's ethical criteria; such attitudes are more reflective of the values of those who walked out during his fiery anniversary speech.

In a 2022 paper by David Gray Widder, Dawn Nafus, Laura Dabbish, and James Herbsleb, the researchers cataloged four main arguments made by open source developers against accepting social responsibility for the tech they create: what I will call the Freedom Zero Argument, the Open Argument, the Hammer Argument, and the Inevitability Argument.

© Coraline Ada Ehmke 2025
C. A. Ehmke, *We Just Build Hammers*, https://doi.org/10.1007/979-8-8688-1249-1_9

Four Reasons Not to Care

[They] sent psychologists out to these people's houses [...] and asked them questions about Ethics so perplexing that even a Jesuit couldn't respond without committing a venial sin.

—Neal Stephenson, *Snow Crash*

The Freedom Zero Argument depends on accepting the Four Software Freedoms as intended by Richard Stallman: as fundamental human rights. Under such an ethos, denying anyone the use of a piece of software is unthinkable, regardless of their intent, and even in cases where their intent is overtly malicious. By this argument, Berkeley's locksmith was innocent: his job was simply to open safes, not to ask whose safe it was or why the stranger wanted it opened.

The Open Argument is based on the belief that free access to source code is a remedy to power imbalances caused by big tech. If everyone has access to source code, which they can freely modify and redistribute, it doesn't matter what the source code is going to be used for. The locksmith may have claimed that the real tragedy of the stranger was that the plans for the top secret superweapon hidden in the safe weren't made public.

The Hammer Argument is based on an interpretation of a quote from Noam Chomsky about technology being neither good nor bad, but simply a neutral tool. The belief in the neutrality of technology is a comforting one, as it completely removes both intent and consequences from the moral equation. But while it's true that a hammer is just a tool, it is also true that some hammers are designed to drive nails and that others are designed specifically to crush skulls. The Hammer Argument is what Berkeley and the Committee on the Social Responsibility of Computer People tried to address when they wrote that some uses of technology are indisputably for the good of society and some are indisputably harmful, even acknowledging that a gray area exists. Under the Hammer argument, the stolen superweapon was just a tool: all the locksmith did was put the tool in someone else's hands.

The Inevitability Argument is a sort of ethical fallacy that posits that harmful technology will be built regardless of an individual choice by a software developer. It recalls the locksmith's justification: that if he didn't accept the stranger's generous offer to open the safe, someone else would. This reasoning is a fallacy because it argues for a moral outcome based on another, hypothetical person's moral decision: this is fine for me to do, because I can imagine someone else thinking it was fine for them to do. This is an attempt at a form of transitive ethics or, as Berkeley might have framed it, a delegation of a responsibility that should never be delegated.

Corporate Capture of Open Source

Hiro feels even at this moment that something has been torn open in the world and that he is dangling above the gap, staring into a place where he does not want to be.

—Neal Stephenson, **Snow Crash**

FOSS was born in response to proprietary software, and from the start, the movement positioned itself as a scrappy defender against the market dominance of a few large tech corporations. Early FOSS practitioners took an adversarial stance toward companies that created proprietary software based on a philosophical disagreement over how software is created, distributed, and controlled.

By the early 2000s, as the rift between Stallman and Eric Raymond continued, both the shortcomings in the ideological purity of Free Software and the weaknesses in the more corporate-friendly approach of open source began to have consequences.

The Four Freedoms as Stallman laid them out were intended as a complete ethical framework, but the benefactors of this framework tended to be other hackers, rather than society as a whole. The emphasis on unlimited freedom revealed the libertarian underpinnings of FOSS and provided the opening that giant tech companies needed to try to co-opt the movement.

The work of the Open Source Initiative, which Raymond had founded with Bruce Perens, helped make open source appear palatable to corporations. But its acceptance came at the expense of giving over authority to the same corporations that were the supposed champions of proprietary software.

With broad adoption of open source came intense pressure on maintainers to keep up with bug reports, code submissions, and feature requests from corporate adopters. Maintainers found themselves victims of their own success. They were not paid for their work, and they relied on volunteer effort to keep their projects alive and relevant. The demand for support that came with large adoptions created a power imbalance that favored the companies who were benefiting from open source at the expense of the very open source communities that were creating it.

The economics of open source caused some maintainers to quit and many projects to fold. In some cases, large or critical open source projects received financial donations from corporate adopters or support from large foundations. For some projects, the majority of source contributions were coming from employees of companies who paid them to work on open source. (At the time of this writing, Intel employees represent the largest single source of contributions to the Linux kernel.)

This created a situation where corporate interests gained undue influence over key projects. The prevalence of the "benevolent dictator for life" model, and the lack of transparent decision-making or governance on most open source projects, raised serious concerns about corporate influence vs. community involvement. Large adoptions brought demand for features that best served the technical road maps of the biggest adopters, who were increasingly leveraging open source components to create commercial products and platforms.

Open source was increasingly playing a role as critical infrastructure for the business of the Internet. Soon, tech giants like Google, Facebook, Amazon, and even Microsoft itself embedded themselves in the open source ecosystem. These companies made billions of dollars in profits based on volunteer effort, with no obligation to give back at all. Open source was attractive in part because it allowed tech companies to outsource both R&D and software development, reducing cost and time to market.

All of this put strain on the philosophy of open source itself, as the behavior of adopters was often out of alignment with the broader ecosystem's principles and values. Permissive licenses had revealed themselves as a double-edged sword. FOSS was supposed to be "free as in speech," but it was fast becoming "free as in labor."

Corruption of the Hacker Ethic

Software [now] comes out of factories, and hackers are, to a greater or lesser extent, assembly-line workers. Worse yet, they may become managers who never get to write any code themselves.

—Neal Stephenson, **SNOW CRASH**

In the early days of computing, the field of programming was an academic and professional pursuit. Most programmers at tech companies came from enviable educational backgrounds and often had advanced degrees in computer science, mathematics, or engineering. Throughout the 1990s, it was standard for companies to require at a minimum a bachelor's degree in computer science to even make it past the first screening of an applicant's resume.

But the Internet was built by hackers, and slowly, large companies started to accept self-taught programmers as well. Many of these autodidactic software developers had grown up in the heyday of the cyberpunk era and had adopted (or adapted) the trappings of the hacker ethic. Now finding themselves employed by tech companies and consequently afforded high salaries, increasingly generous benefits, and even stock options, hackers had to adjust to some degree to the constraints of corporate culture.

Disdain for bureaucracy remained high; the phenomenon of the "pointy-haired boss" harassing, misunderstanding, and mismanaging the programmers who worked for them became a trope. Now that they were on the "inside," they had insight into the inner workings of the corporate machine, which of course invited hacking the institutions themselves. Soon, software engineers found themselves in the C-suite making billion-dollar decisions.

While it's true that the influx of independent-minded and technologically savvy hackers changed the way tech companies operated, the companies changed the hackers, too. Just as cyberpunk authors like Neil Stephenson had warned, capitalism was a force to be reckoned with. Capitalism had a corrosive effect on the hacker ethic itself.

The Hacker Ethic Meets the Protestant Work Ethic

In order to stay alive, you have to spend all day every day doing stupid meaningless work. And the only way to get out of it is to quit, cut loose, take a flyer, and go off into the wicked world, where you will be swallowed up and never heard from again.

—Neal Stephenson, **Snow Crash**

Some scholars have argued that the widespread Protestant work ethic was essential in producing the fertile ground that capitalism needed to take root and flourish in Industrial Age America.

The Protestant work ethic was first named and studied as a phenomenon by German sociologist Max Weber in his 1905 book **The Protestant Ethic and the Spirit of Capitalism**. In the book, Weber credits the Protestant religion's emphasis on work as an act of grace, as a reinvention of the conception of labor.

Weber summarizes the basic tenets of this new labor ethic as "diligence, discipline, and frugality." Work became a "calling" and an act of grace. The belief that prosperity was a sign of divine favor invested the most commonplace manual labor with an aura of nobility, even holiness and intrinsic morality. The resulting willingness to put one's entire conception of self-worth into one's job certainly served the interests of capitalism well.

In 2001, Pekka Himanen, a Finnish philosopher, wrote in **THE HACKER ETHIC AND THE SPIRIT OF THE INFORMATION AGE** that the hacker ethic stood in stark opposition to the Protestant work ethic as described by Weber. Himanen's book, which features an introduction by fellow Finn Linus Torvalds himself, argues that rather than being subjugated by it, hackers are picking the lock of the "iron cage" of capitalism.

Weber observed that once it took root, capitalism needed to rely less and less on the religious justification of its ideal work ethic. Work as an act of grace was soon supplanted by what sociologist Sandra Barns describes as an "achievement ideology," the belief that hard work would always be rewarded, regardless of one's personal circumstances or challenges.

Himanen doesn't recognize how this "achievement ideology" is reflected in the hacker conception of meritocracy, where one's value is commensurate with one's work, regardless of what Torvalds has called "irrelevant" or "distracting" factors like race or gender.

In criticizing the ethic's conception of work as a "calling," Himanen also misses the irony of contrasting the work-obsessed corporate employee with the work-obsessed hacker. In both cases, passion for the work itself is the driving force in life and trumps all other considerations.

Himanen proposes another distinction, that the Protestant work ethic forbids a worker from questioning the nature or impact of their work. This is framed as a tacit surrender to higher authority by Himanen, which is anathema to the hacker. But it is interesting to note that the provenance of Freedom Zero and the insistence on the neutrality of tech are in practice reflections of this Protestant proscription.

Ultimately, as capitalism turned its attention to a new generation of "passionate" technologists, the hacker ethic was subsumed into the Protestant work ethic. This manifested in many ways: accepting the 60-hour work week as normal, admiring those who worked through the night instead of going home to sleep, and glorifying the neglect of social connections in favor of more time spent on code.

In short, they too had been convinced to stake their self-worth on their jobs.

The Centralization of Open

See, the world is full of things more powerful than us. But if you know how to catch a ride, you can go places.

—Neal Stephenson, **Snow Crash**

Hackers entered the workforce in droves, responding to demand driven by the Web 2.0 economy. The company became the community. Large tech corporations attracted the most ambitious developers and soon became hubs that concentrated not only what they considered top-level talent but, most importantly, their networks in the open source world. This contributed not only to a centralization of technologists but to a centralization of influence over open source.

By the late 2000s, it was not unusual for a job applicant to be drilled about their contributions to open source as part of the interview process. In fact, part of the resume screening process in many companies even to this day is checking out a candidate's GitHub profile. But while open source contributions may be an indicator of passion for technology, they're also an indicator of privilege: the overwhelming majority of open source contributors are white men.

When a company hired someone with influence in open source, they knew that employee would inevitably use their influence in connection with their job. The technical needs and priorities of the company became the business of the engineer, and they used their connections accordingly. This allowed employers to exert pressure on the technical road maps of the open source technologies they relied on.

Employees who were passionate about open source naturally welcomed opportunities to open source some of the technologies they were creating as part of their jobs. There were many examples of open source projects originating within a company, including Twitter's Bootstrap user interface library and Facebook's React JavaScript framework.

Companies were willing to share the recipe for some of their internal technologies, but the secret sauce of the dish was kept a secret. The decentralized ecosystem of open source became centralized in a handful of large corporations. The open and the proprietary became intermingled, and tech companies maintained control over both.

All Eyes on the Code

Shit, if I took time out to have an opinion about everything, I wouldn't get any work done.

—Neal Stephenson, **Snow Crash**

The internal technologies that the large tech companies were willing to open source tended to be frameworks or libraries rather than complete programs. FOSS already had a strong culture of making tools for tools, so this approach was broadly welcomed in the community. What's more, aiming a developer's attention on a very specific area of the tech stack kept them focused on small details, rather than the big picture of what their companies were really building.

This specialization and compartmentalization of both the developers and the code that they worked on created a sort of ethical firewall between themselves and the actions of their employers. Insulating developers from larger consequences recalls the subdivision of labor during the Manhattan Project, where an individual engineer had no idea how their piece of work fit into any sort of larger picture.

The pursuit of beautiful code further blurred the open/proprietary boundary, as developers started preemptively architecting their internal code for extractability into open source libraries. A natural side effect of this practice was the standardization of particular architectural patterns that are actually optimized for the unique operating conditions of a particular company. Conway's Law states that the technology an organization produces reflects the internal structure of that organization. Similarly, the open source tooling that an organization produced reflected the internal structure of its technology stack. This had ripple effects on how systems around the world were designed, in some cases even informing or extending protocols and standards.

When a company's idiosyncrasies become an industry standard, it serves to broaden adoption of technologies that conform to their specific business models. For example, by open sourcing their JavaScript framework, Facebook changed the way front-end development was done. React's widespread adoption meant that developers at other companies would be contributing back to a fundamental piece of Facebook's technology stack. As an added bonus, future employees would already be trained in the company's ways of building web applications.

Performing good citizenship in open source also served as a recruiting tool for new hires. Developers naturally wanted to work for companies that embraced open source. Big tech companies started sponsoring open source meetups and conferences, spending extraordinary amounts of time and money courting favor among the attendees at the events and afterparties.

The tech entrepreneur class that had so rapidly risen through the 1990s brought with it the so-called "Californian ideology," uniting the left and the right in a shared distrust of politics and a shared devotion to techno-solutionism. Developers were being encouraged to "move fast and break things." They were given enormous budgets and enormous latitude in what was built and how. The "no-politics-in-tech" attitude espoused by tech founders was a comfort to many, and hyper-specialization kept developers focused and not asking too many questions about the big picture.

With enough eyes on the code, it was almost easy to forget that the company you worked for made its money by spying on people.

Hands Off the Tech

Maybe that's how great warriors do it. Carelessly, not wracking their minds with the consequences.

—Neal Stephenson, **Snow Crash**

The core tenet at the center of both the hacker ethic and its reflection in FOSS was the hands-on imperative, the insistence that everyone should have the freedom to take something apart, understand it, and change how it works. Anyone curious enough about how computers worked could learn to program.

But the software that was being produced by large tech companies was designed to obfuscate the underlying technology as much as possible, hiding the complexity of the way it worked for the sake of nontechnical users. This made reverse-engineering, long a staple in the hacker's toolkit, almost impossible.

Web design tools and web app framework standardization meant that user interfaces across the web pretty much looked and acted the same, increasingly abstracting away the need to understand what was actually happening behind the scenes of an interaction. Internet users came to accept being challenged to prove that they were human by deciphering pixelated characters. They diligently rotated their passwords, accepted default privacy settings, and scrolled quickly to the bottoms of the terms of service pop-ups. They learned the meaning of gear icons and hamburger menus, but forgot the origin of the Save button's floppy disk icon. They were discouraged from asking why they had to perform these complex ceremonies to do something as simple as post a reply on a message board or check on the price of a flight. Where once people worked *on* computers, people now worked *for* computers.

Compared to these increasingly slick but homogenous GUIs, the computers of early hackers became unrecognizable. In designing more and more user-friendly interfaces, hackers were being paid to mediate between the technology and the theoretical end user. The goal was to make it as easy as possible for this person to complete a task in the way that the app provider intended, without having to think about it too much.

The ubiquity of computers had somehow created a dystopia of computer illiteracy. A computer no longer required that someone understand how it worked in order to operate it. Software had abstracted it all away.

As more functionality was hidden from the end user, hardware was also increasingly mystified. More and more computers were no longer designed to be opened by their owners, to have their drives swapped out or to add more RAM. People came to rely on tech that they couldn't repair themselves. And rather than pay exorbitant prices for repairs, the tech became disposable. What couldn't be easily or cheaply repaired would simply be replaced by the latest model.

Meritocracy Falls Flat

In a meritocracy, the best ideas win. In a meritocracy, every-one has access to the same information. Successful work deter-mines which projects rise and gather effort from the community.

— "The Open Source Way," opensource.com

Meritocracy was intended to level the playing field. The idea was that if one was solely judged by the value of their code, divorced from identity, differences like color or gender wouldn't matter at all.

However, meritocracy in the context of FOSS makes an assumption: that everyone who wants to work on open source, can. But everyone doesn't actually start out on a level playing field; in fact, the very differences that meritocracy was intended to erase make all the difference in who is allowed to participate. With a few exceptions, open source had always been dominated by white men. It was white men who tended to have the most free time and the most relaxed day jobs, while it was women whose lower salaries and unpaid labor made it possible for these men to enjoy their free time. In practice, it was only the comfortably well-off white men who had a chance of starting out on equal footing with everyone else.

What's more, many of the people who rose to the top of the meritocratic hierarchy turned out to not be great people. Linus Torvalds was notorious for profanity-laden personal attacks, tearing people down when he thought that their code was inferior. Richard Stallman made problematic statements about topics like rape and underage sex. Eric S Raymond used his blog to tout his gun collection and share his opinions about the intellectual inferiority of Black people.

Beyond the individual participants, meritocracy applied to the projects in the open source ecosystem as well. Developers on different projects were competing for social capital and the job opportunities that it might bring; they had to be strategic about what projects they launched and what projects they contributed to.

The meritocratic philosophy of open source tied status and social currency to adoptions, and the larger the adoption, the better. This created a system of incentives for creating new open source technologies that were specifically designed to appeal to the needs of high-status, large-scale adopters. Developers were shifting from building tools to scratch their own itches to essentially marketing their open source projects to corporate audiences. Success in open source started to involve a lot of blog posts, a lot of podcasts, and a lot of conference talks. Increasingly, it wasn't just the quality of the code that determined social status; it was the quality of the marketing.

Any significant adoption of open source—including the Department of Defense adopting open source drone software for offensive military applications—was seen as a victory for the FOSS movement. The value of the adoption was divorced from its impact on society.

Even in open source, developers were expected to focus on the small details of the code rather than the big picture of how it was being used.

The Price of Free Information

Ubiquitous computing and the free flow of information promised to be an antidote to the tyranny of the expert authority. Everyone could have equal access to any information they needed. The world's knowledge would be laid out for anyone who was curious enough to explore and learn.

In practice, the ubiquity of computers, combined with the erosion of privacy, exposed computer users to unprecedented levels of digital surveillance and data collection. Technologies that were intended to improve the functionality of the web became weaponized against its users.

Browser cookies were an idea that was borrowed from the "magic cookie" of the UNIX world. They were invented at Netscape in 1994, in response to one of the company's ecommerce clients complaining about the amount of data they had to store server-side to maintain user session state. A browser cookie feature would allow a server to store a small amount of data, like a session ID, invisibly on the user's computer. The browser cookie enabled persistent state to be maintained between page loads, enabling functionality like authentication, navigation breadcrumbs, and shopping carts to function.

Unfortunately, cookies could also be set by third parties and used to track users across sites. If sites W, X, and Y included a banner ad or even a tracking pixel from site Z, site Z would be able to set a cookie that could be used to identify an individual user as they moved through pages and between these sites, building an ever-expanding model of a user's interests and behaviors.

When JavaScript hit browsers in 1995, it was intended to allow web developers to create more dynamic sites with interactive elements that worked after the page was loaded. Prior to JavaScript, every web page loaded in a browser was static. JavaScript allowed web pages to be enhanced with interactive components like dynamic form elements, sophisticated navigation widgets, hover states, and even simple animations. But JavaScript also allowed ad providers to serve up ads that were customized to the individual user, mining not just cookie data but even browser history for ad targeting purposes.

By the turn of the century, advertising had come into its own on the web. While web developers battled cross-site request forgery attacks and browser developers debated standards, marketers excitedly talked about CPMs and click-through rates. The bulk sale of ad placements was enabled by early ad networks, soon supplanted by the algorithmically driven ad customization behemoth that was Google AdWords.

By 2009, search histories were routinely mined to drive personalized ads. User data became increasingly valuable, and data harvesting became big business. Google's advertising revenue reached nearly $30 billion by 2010.

Riding the wave of open source, ad-tech companies became some of the biggest proponents of FOSS. From Google to Facebook to Twitter, major advertising companies became major contributors to the open source ecosystem, from financial support to code contributions to complete open source projects of their own. They played a sort of ethical shell-game with developers and employees alike; they were doing all the right things for all the wrong reasons.

Advertising had won the battle for the soul of the Internet. What had started in the 1990s with a single 468×60-pixel banner ad at the top or bottom of a static web page had turned into the online equivalent of Stephenson's dystopian "loglo": a perpetual haze of product ads, logos, and personalities crowding out every bit of content. The search bar took the place of the little blue Internet Explorer icon as the default interface to the web. The Internet had revolted over the market dominance of Microsoft's Internet Explorer, but accepted Google, the largest ad-tech data harvester of all, as its homepage.

Ad-tech had killed the Metaverse.

Computers Were a Mistake

It's a cold clammy reality that she can't do a damn thing about.

—Neal Stephenson, SNOW CRASH

Hackers had firsthand, lived experience with the transformative power of computers. It was only natural to want to distribute that transformative potential as widely as possible. The more people that had access to computers, the better their lives would be.

In reality, computers were changing lives, but not always for the better.

The Internet became a vector for viruses and worms and a sort of automated social engineering hack that came to be called "phishing." Scammers had access to an enviable and ever-growing toolset, from mass spam campaigns to emails requesting the recipient to share credit card numbers or passwords. People were admonished not to click on attachments from unknown senders for fear of infecting their computer, or even their entire workplace's network, with a virus.

Ecommerce was driving so-called brick-and-mortar stores out of business. Amazon, which had killed off first small and then large bookstores, had branched into general merchandise. Soon, building on lessons learned from running their own data centers, Amazon started offering hosting services in the new AWS Cloud. Even data centers, long a lucrative local enterprise for Internet businesses, were under threat from Amazon.

With the advent of Twitter in 2007, social media soon overtook traditional media as a primary source of news and information for millions of people. Ad-tech was finding new pathways into our daily lives. The algorithms driving engagement on social media platforms incentivized incendiary content and manufactured outrage. Developers were duped into building systems that, far from being neutral, actually incentivized antisocial behavior.

While all of this change was happening, as more and more of daily life relied on an Internet connection, the line between the haves and the have nots grew even more starkly defined. The digital divide meant that many people were left behind as the information age raced forward. "Move fast and break things" soon became "move fast and break people."

As hackers made concession after concession to eager product managers, the time would soon come when someone would have to have a PayPal account to do their laundry, install a phone app to use the bathroom in a restaurant, and maintain an Internet connection to turn on their lights.

Reflection

Cyberpunk authors gave technologists a future to fear. Following on the critical media studies of the 1970s and 1980s, researchers and scholars had similarly predicted a future of massive centralization of media and information. The hacker ethic was supposed to be the antidote to all of this. The future was supposed to arrive in a smart pizza box delivered by a sword-wielding Metaverse architect.

But despite their best efforts, hackers couldn't make the world any more rational than the atomic scientists or Berkeley and his peers had before them.

The promise of the Information Age had been the digital transformation of human experience. Unfortunately, in the Silicon Valley context, this transformation had become all about advertising dollars.

But what if the Information Age was less about connecting computers and more about connecting people? What if FOSS could aspire to more than mere neutrality? What if the hacker ethic could be rescued by a new generation of hackers who embraced the other half of Berkeley's vision of the future: social responsibility?

PART IV

An Ambiguous Heterotopia

CHAPTER 10

Trouble on Triton

We've seen the influence of cyberpunk on the days of the early Internet, but to understand what came next, we need to go back a little farther. If writers like Neil Stephenson set the stage for the major conflicts of the 1990s and early 2000s, it was a writer from a previous generation who anticipated the cultural clash that would sweep the tech world in the 2010s. How would cultural conflict impact the future of our tech-enabled society? Could a people-focused, cultural approach address the shortcomings of the hacker era and move us closer to Edmund Berkeley's vision of social responsibility in technology?

Movements Toward Liberation

At the same time that Berkeley was preparing his impassioned speech for the ACM anniversary dinner, and the hackers at MIT's AI Lab prepared to celebrate the tenth anniversary of its founding, people in the United States were taking to the streets: people who were tired of their rights being suppressed.

Following World War II, prosperity in the United States was very unevenly distributed. Women were dismissed from their wartime jobs to return to domestic duties, robbed of most opportunities for a career outside the home. Flight to the suburbs sharpened divisions between the rich and the poor and left urban areas blighted and underfunded. Schools, places of business, and even entire cities were racially segregated according to the principle of "separate but equal." Homosexuality was a criminal offense.

© Coraline Ada Ehmke 2025
C. A. Ehmke, *We Just Build Hammers*, https://doi.org/10.1007/979-8-8688-1249-1_10

As a result of disparities like these, the 1960s and 1970s were a time of massive cultural conflict. There were protests, marches, and civil disobedience actions happening across the country at an unprecedented scale. The fundamental theme of the many movements that came into focus during this time was *liberation*.

Liberation involves the personal, social, and political empowerment of disenfranchised people. Liberation movements of the time included the Civil Rights Movement, Lesbian and Gay Liberation movements, Women's Lib, and the American Indian Movement. People were organizing to challenge the status quo of discrimination and oppression of marginalized communities.

Organizing for social change was nothing new, but something was different this time.

The Politics of Identity

We realize that the only people who care enough about us to work consistently for our liberation are us.

—From the "Combahee River Collective Statement"

Each of the drivers of these distinct liberation movements reflected a facet of identity: identity as a woman, identity as Black or brown, identity as gay or lesbian. This individualization of liberation was captured succinctly in the concept of "identity politics." While the term has since been co-opted and is a pejorative today, the original conception of identity politics represented a significant change in understanding complex sociopolitical dynamics. Rather than organizing around political agendas, people were starting to organize around who they were.

The phenomenon of identity politics emerged through the late 1960s and into the 1970s, and the term itself was first used in a manifesto published by a Black feminist socialist organization called the Combahee

River Collective (named after a military operation in North Carolina run by abolitionist Harriet Tubman that resulted in over 700 slaves being freed). In the statement, the group wrote that "the most profound and potentially most radical politics come directly out of our own identity." Identity politics recognized that certain identities—being Black, being a woman, being gay—subjected people to different forms of discrimination and repression.

Critiques of identity politics focused on its potential for divisiveness, or the danger that it might reinforce things like biological or racial essentialism: categories of being that are imposed from outside based on the expectations of the dominant culture. Later, the idea of intersectionality (which posits that even *combinations* of identities bring with them distinct kinds of oppression) would offer another critique of the movement.

Despite its flaws, identity politics brought focus on promoting self-determination and political equity for groups that are usually excluded from power. Questions of identity defined the era, and this gestalt was reflected in the speculative fiction of the time as well.

Introducing Samuel Delany

Samuel Delany was born to a well-to-do family in Harlem in April of 1942. His grandfather had been born enslaved and after his emancipation became an Episcopalian bishop. Other notable family members included a judge, a poet, and two early civil rights pioneers. His father's comfortable income came from the family funeral home business.

Despite the family's impressive credentials and secure socio-economic status in New York, Delany did not have a good childhood. His father physically abused him, and Delany began routinely running away from home at a very young age. He likely felt further stigmatized in his teen years after his discovery of his own bisexuality.

Delany published his first story, "Salt," in 1960, when he was just 18 years old. He went on to become an award-winning science fiction author, professor, semiotician, and critic, with four Nebula awards, two Hugos, induction into the Science Fiction and Fantasy Hall of Fame, and multiple lifetime achievement awards. He has held various prestigious roles in academia, including teaching at SUNY, the University of Massachusetts, and Temple University.

In science fiction history, Delany is notable for being the first Black and Queer author to win acclaim in the genre. Delany's last name is famously subject to being misspelled in reviews, as "Delaney." The mistake was even made by one of his publishers, who misspelled the name on the title page of one of his books.

Delany has been described as a "liberationist," and rightly so; liberation from classist, racial, gendered, and sexual systems of oppression is a consistent theme in his fiction and nonfiction.

The New Wave

The flashing lights, the dials, and the rest of the imagistic para-phernalia of science fiction functioned as social signs—signs people learned to read very quickly. They signaled technology. And technology was like a placard on the door saying, "Boys Club! Girls, keep out. Blacks and Hispanics and the poor in general, go away!

—Samuel Delany, quoted in an interview with Mark Dery published as "Black to the Future"

Delany is recognized as a prominent example of the "New Wave" movement in science fiction. Along with contemporaries Roger Zelazny, Ursula Le Guin, and Philip K Dick, the writers of this period embraced the experimental, in terms of both themes and forms. Where traditionally the "science" side of science fiction was the most emphasized, New Wave writers incorporated the social sciences into their work, notably language and concepts from psychology, linguistics, and semiotics.

Delany and his fellow writers brought a thoughtful and literary depth to a field made famous by pulp, but the genre remained inferior in the eyes of "serious" literary critics.

Delany is regarded as the first science fiction author to frankly address human sexuality in all of its varieties. His novels depict a future of innately complex identities wrestling with sociopolitical, socio-technological precarity. His Blackness, his feminism, and his Queerness are woven into the fabric of his worlds.

His characters are often barefoot or even missing a shoe and very matter-of-factly sporting what we would consider outlandish fashions. He depicts a staggering fluidity and plurality of gender expressions, sexualities, and identities. It is not unprecedented for characters in his novels to change their orientation, or even their sex, over the course of a story.

In a 2023 profile for **NEW YORKER** magazine titled "How Samuel Delany Reimagined Sci-Fi, Sex, and the City," writer Julian Lucas credits the 1984 volume of Delany's "Nevèrÿon" series as being the first novel to address the then-rampant AIDS epidemic. He describes the story as interleaving the fantasy novel with "disquieting scenes from the streets of contemporary New York," mirroring in fiction the horrors of the disease and, most importantly, how society was dealing (and not dealing) with that horror. Every sex act portrayed in the book was one that had been deemed safe against the transmission of AIDS in the real world, and an appendix to the novel was more explicit in providing practical advice for avoiding the disease. Delany never had another sci-fi novel published by a major house again.

Themes of race, gender, and sexuality supersede the technological in his writing, but technology is still central to his stories. Future societies, whether on earth or in space, rely on fantastical technology to meet their basic needs and provide for their survival. There are always indications that the tech surrounding his characters is incredibly advanced but also taken for granted.

But the most prominent technology in Delany's work, broadly speaking, is language.

The Language of the Future

In the introduction to **A JEWEL-HINGED JAW**, a book of Delany's essays, writer Matthew Cheney recalls the author reflecting on what makes science fiction special. For Delany, it's not the "gadgets and landscapes," but rather the use and interpretation of language, by both the writer and the reader, that distinguishes the genre.

Delany is a student of semiotics, and this is reflected in his work. The social science of semiotics deals with the study of signs: signifiers, which encode a concept, and the signified, the concept being communicated. Semiotics posits systems of transmitting and interpreting signs and signals as a communication technology, one that can manifest in fashion or visual design as easily as in written language.

In **BABEL**-17, published in 1966, Delany explored language-as-technology explicitly. Babel-17 was the name given to the alien language that was being used as a tactical weapon against humanity. The protagonist of the story, Rydra Wong, is a spaceship captain, linguist, and poet who learns the language to defend humanity from the alien invaders. But with her fluency comes a psychic transformation that frees her mind from its human constraints, allowing her to transcend the conflict.

This is a fictionalized exploration of the theory of linguistic relativity, more commonly known as the Sapir–Whorf hypothesis. The theory posits that the vocabulary and syntax of an individual's native language shapes and constrains the way that they think and solve problems. While the theory is controversial, there is evidence that supports at least some of its claims. Regardless, its core conception is fascinating fodder for science fiction, and Delany explores it to great effect.

But Delany is not simply employing semiotics or linguistics as a literary device. He's literally using language to hack the way that we, as readers, understand the world around us, by providing a vocabulary (signifiers) and corresponding set of concepts (the signified) that challenge our preconceptions.

The emphasis that Delany puts on the significance of language as a technology anticipates Neil Stephenson's "hieroglyphs," discussed in Chapter 7. The deliberate creation of new forms of iconic shorthand for new conceptions in science fiction was necessary to move the genre beyond the shiny rayguns and alien worlds of its golden age.

In the essay "Critical Methods/Speculative Fiction," Delany quotes an **OXFORD DICTIONARY** editor as saying that science fiction was the most prolific genre in terms of lasting contributions to the English language. The appearance of new words from science fiction superseded that of poetry by the 1930s. The future was being shaped by the words invented to describe that future.

Delany used the language of science fiction as a liberatory force to lift people out of prevailing forms of control. Perhaps for this reason, Delany has stated that a science fiction story is not a prophecy: it is an incantation.

Feminism in Science Fiction

Who made man the exclusive judge, if woman partake with him the gift of reason?

—Mary Wollstonecraft, **VINDICATION OF THE RIGHTS OF WOMAN**

In the mid-1960s, Delany lived with his partner Marilyn Hacker in an apartment in the East Village of New York City. Hacker, not yet the award-winning poet and critic that she would one day be, was working as a copyeditor at Ace Books, a publisher specializing in niche genres like science fiction. Hacker often came home from work and reported in to Delany on the latest atrocious representation of women in the stories she was working with.

Things hadn't changed much since the Golden Age depictions of female characters as either damsels in distress or mere adornments in service of their handsome heroes. Delany and his generation of science fiction writers were determined to do better.

Delany and Hacker had long conversations on the extent to which the sexism of the culture was reflected in literature. They talked about the unwritten literary conventions, unfortunately mirrored even in speculative fiction, that constrained how women were allowed to be portrayed in popular media.

In his "Letter to the Symposium on 'Women in Science Fiction' under the Control, for Some Deeply Suspect Reason, of One Jeff Smith," Delany reflected on this time, relating a series of conversations about the problems with how women were typically represented. Finally, he and Hacker arrived at a set of criteria defining how best to portray realistic female characters in fiction.

First, the character must be shown to make three types of actions: "purposeful" actions that move the plot forward, "habitual" actions that reveal character, and "gratuitous" actions that point to the character's life outside of the current narrative. While male characters were typically allotted all three, Hacker suggested that there were only two archetypes for women in fiction, the "evil bitch" and the "simp," both ugly clichés. In the first case, the character was allowed only purposeful actions, permitting no depth or life outside her villainy. In the latter case, the character was neither effectual nor complex, performing only gratuitous actions in service of stronger characters. Truly three-dimensional female characters, they agreed, must act in ways that demonstrate agency, individuality, and wholeness.

Second, the character's so-called "economic anchors" must be clearly demonstrated. The reader should know about her job, where her money comes from, and what degree of economic freedom she enjoys. Without these details, it is impossible to place the character in relation to the socio-economic context of the society portrayed in the story. Complexities of experience with class are intertwined with experiences of race, gender, and sexuality in Delany's worlds.

The third requirement for realistic female characters is relational. She must have believable relationships with other female characters in the story. These relationships can be friendly, adversarial, professional, or any combination, but they must reflect the complexity of the characters and the world in which they live. This anticipates the Bechdel–Wallace test that was conceived in 1985: in order to pass the test, a work of film or fiction must depict a conversation between women on any subject that does not involve men.

Finally, effective characters of all genders must have a real problem to solve and not simply a romantic one. While Delany certainly allows for romance (and sex) in his novels, the romantic subplots must always be considered in service to the greater narrative.

Delany saw that science fiction, as a marginalized genre, granted authors greater latitude than traditional literature in terms of what sort of characters are permitted. Why then couldn't science fiction be used to counter the prevailing literary narratives about women?

Delany came to be known for unique depictions of female characters in possession of agency and purpose, demonstrating a depth of character that was nearly unprecedented. His work challenged notions of who was allowed to be a hero(ine) in imaginings of the future.

In both his fiction and nonfiction, Delany engaged with feminist theory as part of a broader, intersectional exploration of identity and marginalization. He didn't stop at challenging the portrayal of women in fiction: he tackled issues around race, ethnicity, gender, and sexuality with equal fervor. Delany's work took the principles, values, and desired outcomes of the feminist, gay liberation, and antiracism movements of the time and projected them into the far future.

The Father of Afrofuturism

In 1994, scholar and media critic Mark Dery published an essay called "Black to the Future," a piece on Black themes in science fiction. He had interviewed three prominent thinkers for the article: writer Samuel Delany, critic Greg Tate, and scholar Tricia Rose.

The essay is credited with coining the term "Afrofuturism" to describe the cultural phenomenon of a science fiction framing of the historical reality of the African diaspora. The term Afrofuturism as it relates to a cultural and philosophical aesthetic is applied not only to works of fiction but also art, music, fashion, and philosophy.

Afrofuturism explores the legacy of the violent colonization, uprooting, and cultural destruction of the people of the African continent as it applies to imaginings about the future. It presents an optimistic view of the potential of culture and technology to interweave in ways that are respectful of the past, acknowledge the present, and embrace the future. In its science fiction representations, Afrofuturism challenges classic science fiction tropes of worlds populated by life in every skin color but Black.

Dery cited Samuel Delany and Octavia Butler (a former student of Delany's who became a literary giant in her own right) as some of the few Black science fiction writers tackling themes of Black futures, placing him at the head of the critical literary movement of Afrofuturism.

A later profile published in the **New Yorker** quoted Delany himself, however, describing Afrofuturism as "well-intentioned" but fundamentally a marketing tool.

Marginalized at the Outset

Chip Delany is right: it exists.

—Ursula Le Guin on "paraliterature," quoted in
Conversations with Ursula K. Le Guin, edited by Carl
Howard Freedman

Delany believes that science fiction is uniquely positioned as a catalyst for social change, by virtue of its marginalization. Science fiction is an example of what he calls "paraliterature," the sorts of works that critics ignore or look down upon as mere entertainment, and not worth considering for their cultural value.

He describes paraliterature as being a form of social division. If you go to a typical bookstore, he asks, where have the staff placed the science fiction books? Certainly not on the table displays in the front of the store or, for that matter, in the shelves of "acceptable" literature. Science fiction, horror, and fantasy are deliberately located in the least accessible places in the stores: the back wall, an obscure corner, the low shelves. The staff can be secure in the knowledge that fans of books like these will seek them out wherever they are and no one else will care.

While many sci-fi authors begrudge the literary world for ignoring an entire genre of fiction, Delany sees this predilection as the perfect cover for introducing dangerous ideas that challenge the status quo. It is the literary obscurity to which the genre is banished that makes it such a powerful force for change.

In an interview for the publication **PARA•DOXA**, reprinted in the collection **SHORTER VIEWS**, Delany called for the deliberate introduction of "markers," or expressions of cultural values, into science fiction writing, as a form of influencing or guiding the ongoing development of culture. With thoughtfully designed markers, he reasoned, values that we want to encourage are embedded in a futuristic context as a vehicle for transmission to the broader culture. Delany sees the power of using language as a way of changing the world, with fictional worlds providing a backdrop for a thoughtful exercise in future-building.

To Delany, the marginalization of paraliterary genres like science fiction (or, for that matter, comic books and porn) is where they derive their power. Writing it and reading it are by definition countercultural. "[Paraliterature] is always at its most honest and most effective," he wrote, "when it operates from the margins."

Delany on Wells

Bear in mind that the novel—no matter how intimate, psychological, or subjective—is always a historical projection of its own time.

—Samuel Delany

In his collection of essays **A Jewel-Hinged Jaw**, Delany credited H.G. Wells for his future histories, but noted that Wells was very much a product of his society. And as his own work showed, speculative fiction, no matter how alien or bizarre the landscape, always reflects the norms, fears, and hopes of a particular place and time.

Delany identified what he referred to as Wells's "twin Victorian views" of technology: that technological progress moves in an orderly, straight line and that human nature with regard to technology is consistent across times and places. He also half-jokingly criticized Wells for his assumption that human history would continue that much further from the present day.

The linearity of human experience is characteristic of the future histories that Wells wrote, as well as his nonfiction. Wells, Delany said, employed a sort of "socially functional logic": the only futures worth exploring are those that are possible, because it's useless to ponder the social impact of the impossible. Delany posited instead that technical and artistic achievements are more of a web of intersecting lines of development whose social impact was fascinating and unpredictable.

Wells's Law asks us to imagine what would happen to the world if one novel thing became true—but that thing, however fantastical, must be something that seems within the realm of possibility. Delany, in his own fiction, turns this logic on its head, asking essentially, "What would be required to sustain a reality in which this impossible thing were true?"

Utopias and Dystopias

In his 1968 novel **N**ova, Delany anticipated human-pluggable computers almost two decades before *Neuromancer* brought cyberpunk to the forefront of science fiction. Where cyberpunk seemed to ignore the sociological nuances of the New Wave generation's work, it certainly picked up on the realistic depictions of the grittiness of the world.

But no matter how bleak some of the futures that Delany writes about may be, his work certainly isn't dystopian.

Of course, cyberpunk didn't invent dystopia. After all, Aldous Huxley's **BRAVE NEW WORLD** was published in 1932, and George Orwell's 1984 followed in 1949. Cyberpunk simply digitized the human wasteland that had been so shockingly portrayed for decades before.

Delany has written that science fiction must transcend the utopia/dystopia divide and find "a more fruitful model" for the development of human society. In "Critical Methods/Speculative Fiction," he complains that the literary criticism directed at science fiction seems obsessed with assessing works in utopia-vs.-dystopia terms. He would prefer that science fiction critics paid attention instead to "all these mythic views of the world" that the genre provides.

In his interview with Mark Dery, Delany reflected on the subgenre of cyberpunk and wondered aloud about its value in the larger universe of speculative fiction. It was not a very positive assessment: he declared that it's fundamentally a "pervasive misreading" of urban technoculture that is unacceptable in the post-Rodney King era.

Despite his reservations about the long-term impact of cyberpunk, he credits William Gibson, a personal friend, with bringing enough attention to science fiction with **NEUROMANCER** that it was elevated to a position, if not of literature, at least worthy of consideration as such.

Paraliterature in Four Colors

Dick [Giordano] had some very special help in the person of Samuel R. Delany—known to his friends as Chip. If you read science fiction, you probably already know Chip, author of 10 books and winner of no less than five major awards. This is Chip's first comic book. We're hoping it won't be his last.

—Denny O'Neil, in the editorial column of *Wonder Woman* #202

Another example of the paraliterary form that Delany promotes as a force for change is the comic book. His first contribution to the field of comics came in 1972, when he wrote the introduction for the trade paperback edition of *Green Lantern/Green Arrow*, a historic volume that addressed racism in the United States heads-on.

The cover of the book showed three comic panels. An old Black man approaches the green-clad Green Lantern. He says that he's read about the superhero's protection of the "blue skins" and rescue of the "orange skins," but that he has neglected Black skins. He challenges Green Lantern to answer why, to which the humbled hero responds, "I ... can't." It was the kind of question that had never been posed before.

The back cover of the book was equally hard-hitting. It shows Green Lantern standing in front of pictures of Dr. Martin Luther King, Jr. and Robert F. Kennedy and decrying the assassinations of a "good black man in Memphis" and a "good white man in Los Angeles." Green Lantern declares that something is wrong, that a moral cancer is "rotting our very souls." The banner above the image promised that the book contained "the most daring dialogue" ever to appear in comics.

The writers were saying that the conventional archetype of the superhero was incapable of dealing with messy, complex, but critical social issues; a new type of hero was needed.

Samuel Delany vs. Gloria Steinem

Women are just a little less willing to put up with certain kinds of shit than men—simply because the concept of a certain kind of shit-free Universe is, in that equally bizarre Jungian abstraction, the female "collective unconscious," too new and too precious.

—Samuel Delany, **Trouble on Triton**

In their 2012 paper "Wonder Woman Wears Pants: Wonder Woman, Feminism and the 1972 'Women's Lib' Issue," researcher Ann Matsuuchi tells the story of how journalist and feminist activist Gloria Steinem and Samuel Delany tangled in a Wonder Woman reboot gone awry. It is a story rife with irony, describing a conflict between an icon of second-wave feminism and a Queer Black feminist writer critiquing that feminism for its exclusion of Black perspectives.

On July 1, 1972, Steinem published the first issue of **Ms. Magazine**, a magazine dedicated to being a voice for women, by women. The magazine's debut cover featured a full-color illustration of a gigantic Wonder Woman in her star-spangled bikini, in the middle of a stride a city block long. She's carrying an entire neighborhood of suburban houses in her lasso, rescuing them from the war-torn landscape in the background. A banner proclaims, "Wonder Woman for President!"

Wonder Woman had famously given up her supernatural powers and her costume, in 1968, when the love of a mortal man bound her to earth while her fellow Amazons departed the planet. With that, she had given up the uniform and reinvented herself as a secret agent along the lines of the "Emma Peel" character from the popular 1960s Avengers series, right down to the hairstyle. The **Ms.** cover hearkened back to the Silver Age era of Wonder Woman that the girls of Steinem's generation had grown up with.

From the start, Wonder Woman was intended as a feminist role model. The character's creators, William Marston, his wife Elizabeth Marston, and their mutual partner Olive Byrne, created Wonder Woman at the height of World War II, adding her to a growing pantheon of iconic women (like Rosie the Riveter) intended to inspire the women of America to their patriotic duties. "Golden Age" Wonder Woman was an Amazon warrior disguised as a war volunteer and often battled villains with comically sinister names like "Professor Menace" and "Baron Blitzkrieg." In a nod to the ladies' ladies, she often used "Great Sappho!" as an exclamation of surprise, a reference to the ancient Greek poet whose works famously described romantic lesbian love.

The plots of the stories were intended to draw attention to gender issues through power inversions and role reversals, often involving bondage themes. Her trademark Lasso of Truth was inspired by Marston's own real-life contribution to crime-fighting: the lie detector.

But by 1968, sales of Wonder Woman comics were at an all-time low, and DC was preparing to shut the book down for good. An editor/writer duo, Mike Sekowsky and Denny O'Neil, were brought on in a last-ditch attempt to save the title. The pair had previously worked together on the progressive Green Lantern series and were trusted with enough latitude to reimagine Wonder Woman to appeal to a new generation of readers. Issue 179, published in December, featured a cover illustration of a black-haired Diana Prince leaving her Amazonian family behind. She'd abandoned her patriotic uniform for a strappy black-and-green dress, a look straight off the Mod streets of London.

The reboot saved Wonder Woman, and the reimagined heroine embarked on a new series of adventures in an arc spanning several years. O'Neil eventually replaced Sekowsky as editor, and for the first issue under his name, he brought in Samuel Delany as writer. The first issue of their collaboration, October 1972's Issue 202, also marked the first time that a Black character was featured in a Wonder Woman comic.

The second issue that Delany wrote was intended as the first in a six-part series. When Issue 203 hit stores in December, the cover featured a white-clad Wonder Woman arriving bursting onto the scene in a darkened warehouse. Accompanied by five wolflike dogs, she races to rescue her friend Cathy Perkins, a fashionably dressed blonde who is hog-tied and propped against a crate on the floor below.

In the story, the down-and-out heroine has just witnessed the love of her life, longtime romantic interest Steve Trevor, gunned down in a mission gone awry. She crashes with a friend who's heavily involved in the Women's Lib movement and gets involved in a conflict between young women working at a department store and their villainous boss and his thugs.

The series was intended to bring Wonder Woman up-to-date with the issues of the day, such as the discrimination that young women entering the workforce were facing. But rather than an abrupt awakening to social issues, Delany plotted out a storyline over which Wonder Woman, now completely living as her alter ego Diana Prince, would be gradually won over from her nationalistic mindset to something that the young women of 1972 could better relate to. In a controversial panel, still early in her social consciousness journey, Diana Prince declares that she's uncertain about Women's Lib and complains that "in most cases," she didn't even like women. The issue ends with a group of Black women confronting the Women's Lib activists over the loss of their own hard-won jobs at the department store.

The response by Steinem to what she interpreted as an antifeminist Wonder Woman was immediate and powerful. Without the context of the overall story arc, it looked like Steinem was right. She didn't know that Delany had written the climax of the series as a battle against antiabortion goons outside a women's health clinic. She didn't know that Delany was offering an intersectional critique of how white, racist, and classist the feminism of the 1970s was. The series was abruptly canceled, and **Ms. Magazine** celebrated their victory and the return of classic Wonder Woman.

The fundamental conflict between Steinem's white feminism and Delany's Black feminism reflected a common criticism of identity politics: the problem of not recognizing the particular challenges faced by people at the intersection of multiple identities.

Issue 204, which came out in February of 1973, was titled "The Second Life of the Original Wonder Woman" and saw the character returned to her iconic patriotic uniform. Thus ended Delany's career as a comic book author.

Enter Sandman

Despite the debacle with Steinem, Delany's belief in the power of comic books remained strong. In 1993, Neil Gaiman invited him to write the introduction to *A Game of You*, an installment of Gaiman's **SANDMAN** series of graphic novels.

Gaiman is never one to shy away from difficult but powerful stories, and **A GAME OF YOU** was no exception. The novel follows a woman named Barbie, who in her dreams finds herself strangely entangled in a surreal world built around the stories of her friends and neighbors. One of these friends is a young transgender woman named Wanda. As Wanda's story unfolds, we see a woman struggling with self-identity while also struggling to survive in a world that seems designed to do her harm. In the end, the world wins, and Wanda meets a horrifying and tragic fate.

Delany's introduction to the story focused on Wanda's subplot and warned against an overly political reading of her story. "The problem with political readings," he wrote, is that "the large and general tend to overwhelm the subtle and specific."

Still, he acknowledges that the rules of the dominant culture always call for members of oppressed groups to be killed off at the end of a story, so that they can be dutifully mourned and quickly forgotten.

Trouble on Triton

A few short years after the Wonder Woman incident, Delany published his 12th novel, **TRITON** (later reprinted as **TROUBLE ON TRITON**). The novel is a complex depiction of racial, sexual, and gender divisions in a technology-fueled war between competing cultural and political philosophies.

In the twenty-second century, humanity has spread out from the inner planets of Earth and Mars to various moons of the gas giants on the other side of the asteroid belt. Planetary culture is an anachronism, a curiosity that belongs to the past. It is rooted in a history too dense to allow for thoughts of the future. Cultural preservation was the planetary imperative; cultural proliferation was the signature of the Satellite societies.

The protagonist is an unlikeable individual named Bron, who lives, works, and wanders the city of Tethys on the titular remote moon of Neptune. Over the course of a few ordinary days, Bron interacts with a dizzying diversity of personalities, from bestial biohackers to a theatre troupe that performs for audiences of one.

Bron moves through the story like a tourist in his own life. He demonstrates a remarkable lack of self-awareness and inflicts casual harm on the people around him, especially the women, who in turn he gets fired, sexually harasses, and falls pathetically in love with.

Bron seems to resent the plurality and fluidity of the people around him. A trip to the more conservative Earth exposes him to the twin perils of a Kafka-esque interrogation of which he may never speak and an elaborately catered dinner date at an old-fashioned, very exclusive hillside restaurant somewhere in Outer Mongolia.

The cold war being waged between Triton and the other Satellite societies and the planetary forces of Earth and Mars comes in and out of focus, mostly relegated to the background but punching through the narrative in scenes of torture and terrorism. No shots are really fired, but the infrastructure that each civilization depends upon is surgically targeted for sabotage to do the maximum damage to its respective hosts.

The war ends with a victory for the Satellites. The cost in human lives numbers in the millions, and Earth and Mars are more or less permanently devastated.

As writer C. Riley Snorton noted about **TROUBLE ON TRITON** in his critical essay "An Ambiguous Heterotopia," the premise of the book is that difference is a common good. He points to the interweaving of technology and identity in the biocentrism of the society that Delany portrays. Any sort of surgical modification can be carried out in less than half an hour, from organ removal to chromosomal editing.

After the war is won, Bron experiences an existential crisis when he realizes that the sort of woman who is attracted to the sort of man that he is—one of the most powerful and important types of men, all things considered—was nearly extinct. In an act of self-sacrifice, he goes to a sex change clinic to become one of those women. His gender transformation isn't a matter of identity; it is a practical strategy for propagating conservatism. He even objects to the intake clinician prematurely referring to him as "Ms. Bron." Seventeen minutes or so later, the job is done. Bron is now free to find and mate with her Übermensch.

There are literally dozens of legally and socially recognized genders on Triton, and the parameters for one's sexual attractions are programmable. But out of the proliferation of available orientations, expressions, and identities, Bron selected the most conservative archetype possible in his society: the chromosomally cisgender, hormonally heterosexual, factory-issue female. He does this, he believes, for the future of the species and specifically for the good of other men like him.

The Modular Calculus

Bron works as a metalogician, practicing a sort of advanced symbolic logic or mathematics called the "modular calculus," a science too arcane for even advanced experts like him to fully comprehend. The modular calculus analyzes and prescribes the conditions upon which modern life is built. The machinery powered by Bron's metalogical calculations is never seen, never discussed; it is part of the ambient techno-social landscape on Triton.

The complexities of the modular calculus are necessary for modeling, predicting, and directing the behavior of an infinitely diverse population of irrational human beings. It is Delany's incarnation of the idea of imposing rational thought on social order, a theme we've seen repeated throughout the work of Wells, Berkeley, and Stephenson.

Delany seems to say that without rational underpinnings, however arcane or almost magical, society can only succumb to chaos. It is the ambient bureaucracy of the Satellites that makes a place of difference possible. Overt bureaucracy is only suitable for places of conformity.

Rather than writing the story to answer the Wellsian question of "what would happen if this thing were true," **TROUBLE ON TRITON** asks "what would need to be true for this thing to happen?" Rather than adhering to the conservative convention of focusing on the possible, Delany posits that only a society sophisticated enough to harness a technology like the modular calculus can sustain such a variety of cultures and identities.

The culture of Triton prioritizes fluidity of identity and the sanctity of subjective reality. It is the novel's most poignant irony that the ultimately conservative Bron was essentially a technician on the machinery that made the diversity and flexibility of life on Triton politically, culturally, and technologically possible.

The Stars Are Different

Planetary life is a toxic blend of oppressive bureaucracy and tasteless consumerism that meld into a bland near-utopia. Earth and Mars operated on an economy of nostalgia that was sustained by technology, convention, and violence.

On the Satellite moons like Triton, society is a "heterotopia" built around institutions, relationships, and intersections of difference. (The term is not used explicitly within the text, but appears in the subtitle of the novel as "An Ambiguous Heterotopia.") The Satellites operated on an economy of communal love, sex, labor, and art that was sustained by an almost fractal diversity of identities.

The conflict in **TROUBLE ON TRITON** is essentially the conflict between a return to the "innocence" of life on Earth, with all its anachronistic conformity, and the embrace of a future among the stars, with all its infinite recombinations. The conformity of life on solid ground was part of the attraction for some, while irrational and repellant for others, who felt most at home with a sort of pragmatic diversity too ingrained to be consciously noticed. It is the fundamental cultural struggle between homogeneity and heterogeneity: sameness and difference. Delany is warning us that if we accede to conformity, we will never outgrow the world we already know.

Reflection

The future that Delany offers up in **TROUBLE ON TRITON** is grittily realistic without being dystopian. It is devilishly complicated but efficiently executed. It is occasionally frightening, but somehow simultaneously liberatory. The magic required to make this possible is deeply embedded in the technology evolving in concert with culture.

One of the underlying questions in Delany's work is: what techno-social systems need to be in place to support and sustain a technologically advanced society with an almost infinite number of identities?

In the next chapter, we'll see how this question became central to a modern liberation struggle playing out on the Internet, the tech justice movement of the 2010s.

CHAPTER 11

The Modular Calculus

By the 2010s, open source was well-established; some even said that it had "eaten the world." Free and open source software was widely accepted as a viable and thriving ecosystem by most of the tech industry. Even Microsoft became an active participant in open source, with its own set of licenses approved by the Open Source Initiative, public collaborations with the Linux community, and membership in the Apache Foundation. The old rivalries were forgotten by some but held onto with deep distrust by others.

New technologists were showing up in droves in response to the increasing demand for software developers across almost all sectors of the economy. A growing wave of developers wanted the same access to prosperity that the hackers of the 1990s and 2000s unexpectedly found themselves enjoying. They were excited about meaningful, challenging, and well-paying careers and the opportunity to participate in the burgeoning startup culture. They were pursuing dreams of contributing to the incredible breakthroughs in tech that, it seemed, would never end.

An Identity Crisis in Tech

Some of the people entering the tech industry had different sets of values, different backgrounds, and different life experiences than those who had come before them. As the tech industry began to become more diverse, some of the assumptions that went unchallenged in what had been a largely homogeneous community faced scrutiny or even became sources of contention and conflict. The changes that were happening

© Coraline Ada Ehmke 2025
C. A. Ehmke, *We Just Build Hammers*, https://doi.org/10.1007/979-8-8688-1249-1_11

caught many people off guard and made some of them quite defensive about the validity, and even viability, of their subculture. Navigating these conflicts wouldn't be easy for anyone and often brought out the worst in human nature.

The barriers they faced put the impetus on the new generation of technologists to adapt the hacker ethic not just for the benefit of society but for their own survival. They would need ingenuity, curiosity, and determination to prepare the way for the kind of thriving, infinitely diverse future society imagined by writers like Delany. A future that had people like them in it.

The Future Comes Under Attack

We perceived that, in these genre texts, there existed an aspect of 'science' and an aspect of 'fiction,' and because of the science, something about the fiction was different.

—Samuel Delany, **TROUBLE ON TRITON**, Appendix A

For the past few decades, conventions around who was "allowed" to write science fiction and who was "allowed" to read it had been changing. The diversification of narratives, authors, and audiences that had begun with the New Wave writers was starting to be reflected in the new faces in the tech scene. In fact, this shift in science fiction had probably inspired a lot of people to pursue tech in the first place, even when society—like Delany's blinking lights and dials warning away girls, the poor, and anyone who was Black or Brown—said there was no place for them there.

The 2010s also saw the rise of a dangerous contingent of people who didn't like how things were changing in open source, gaming, science fiction, and other areas of geek culture. They felt besieged by progressive ideas, they didn't like having their privilege challenged, and they were too invested in the status quo to have much of an appetite for social change.

In many ways, they reflected the attitude of regressive, anachronistic conformity that the citizens of Earth and Mars had in **TROUBLE ON TRITON**. And, like the Earthlings and Martians in the book, they waged war against change using tactics of terror and sabotage.

In 2015, some members of this contingent became so incensed at what they considered leftist politics in science fiction that they decided to throw a monkey wrench into the Hugo Awards, one of the most prestigious awards in sci-fi and fantasy. During the award's nomination period, a large and loosely organized brigade of so-called "Sad Puppies" and "Rabid Puppies" waged an online campaign to overwhelm the organization's voting system and drown out the voices and votes of legitimate participants. They tried to rig the system to ensure that awards went to authors whose right-leaning politics they found more appropriate to the future that they wanted for themselves. Their rallying cry was that so-called "identity politics" had no place in science fiction or anywhere else for that matter.

They managed to create a lot of chaos and disruption but ultimately failed to accomplish what they had set out to do. However, they had established themselves as a cultural and technological force to be reckoned with and managed to attract the attention of other right-leaning people, both in and out of tech.

The Sad and Rabid Puppies movement persisted in various forms as late as 2018, but most of their adherents had long since returned their attention to other perceived battlefronts: gaming and programming.

The Alt-Right Storms the Internet

The attack on the Hugo Awards was part of a larger backlash against the changes that were taking place in geek culture. The ideals of the alt-right found fertile ground among the kinds of people who felt threatened by these changes. The connection between the discontent geeks and the rising right-wing culture in the United States became clear during a period known as Gamergate.

By 2014, independent game developers started producing innovative and entertaining games that were able to compete with even the largest gaming studios. Games were emerging as a new form of paraliterature, a technological platform for storytelling.

This new style of indie games created alternatives to popular genres like first-person shooters or MMORPGs and attracted a more diverse group of players. For some, games like these were perceived as an ideological attack on (male-dominated) gaming culture by proponents of identity politics.

One game that came under attack was called **DEPRESSION QUEST**, created in 2013 by Zoë Quinn, Patrick Lindsey, and Alex Lifschitz. The game, developed with the Twine engine, put the player in the role of an outwardly happy but inwardly profoundly depressed main character. The action in the game involved simply performing everyday activities and conducting basic social interactions. But the options for dialog or other choices are visibly filtered through a lens of depression in the game interface.

When the game hit Steam, a group of right-leaning members of the gamer community went berserk. Among other allegations, Quinn was accused of sleeping with a game critic to secure a good review. (This was a patently false charge, as the critic they named had never even reviewed **DEPRESSION QUEST**.) The flames were fanned when Quinn's former partner disclosed details of their relationship in a public blog post.

Quinn found themselves receiving death threats mailed to their home address, hounded on every platform, and the subject of an alarmingly intense campaign of harassment, abuse, and terrifying death threats. The attacks soon spread to other alternative voices in gaming, including media critic Anita Sarkeesian (who produced a "Tropes vs. Women in Video Games" series) and game developer Brianna Wu.

The "Gamergaters" organized their efforts using chan boards, a style of bulletin board favoring long threads filled with memes. Initially, Gamergaters used 4chan and Reddit as their home bases, eventually migrating to 8chan after a dispute with 4chan admins over doxing. Some took refuge on Kiwi Farms, a chan board founded by Joshua Moon in 2013, which facilitated targeted campaigns against transgender technologists and game developers (who they referred to as troons, or "tranny goons"). At least three of the trans women targeted by the site were driven to suicide.

Publicly, the rallying cry of Gamergate was "ethics in game journalism!" But on the chan boards, some of the most hateful places on the Internet, their true motivations were stated in plain sight.

Their violent campaign against progressive themes in games attracted widespread media coverage. Not all of it favored the victims of abuse. Alt-right figure Milo Yiannopoulos, who covered technology for Trump advisor Steve Bannon's **BREITBART NEWS**, did his best to whip up fervor and recruit more people to the Gamergate cause.

Some years later, Bannon bragged in his memoir that Yiannopoulos had effectively created Trump's very own personal online army.

The Tech Justice Movement

The conflict soon spilled over into the broader tech ecosystem. There were plenty of targets. With progress in the tech industry toward more diversity, some of the fundamental ideals championed by social activists in preceding decades—feminism, antiracism, and acceptance of gender and sexuality minorities—took hold in the emerging generation of technologists, and they were not shy about their convictions.

Many of these newcomers were entering an industry, and a culture, that wasn't designed for them. They suffered microaggressions in the workplace and macroaggressions on social media. They endured racism, sexism, homophobia, and transphobia at work and online. Targeted for their identities, they were living proof of the old slogan from the identity politics days that "the personal is always political."

Statistics on employment in the industry, gathered in 2016, told part of the story. Women in tech were paid at least 28% less than male peers with the same qualifications and were employed at half their rate. They made up less than 11% of Silicon Valley executives. One in four women in tech had experienced being sexually harassed at work and were twice as likely as men to drop out of tech altogether citing workplace and culture issues. The situation was even worse for women who were also Black or brown or transgender.

The people who were challenging the status quo in tech often found themselves driven from jobs, demonized, harassed, threatened, and abused. The backlash drove a lot of good people out of tech. But it also mobilized a small group of technologists determined to leverage their skills and positions to advocate for much-needed change in the industry despite the personal cost. This made them targets but also made them the heroines of a new chapter in the history of ethics in computing.

The alt-right preferred the term "social justice warrior."

Dawn of the Social Justice Warriors

Political commitment isn't a perimeter, Sam; it's a parameter.

—Samuel Delany, **Trouble on Triton**

On October 7, 2015, the **Washington Post** published an article by Abby Ohlheiser titled "Why 'social justice warrior,' a Gamergate insult, is now a dictionary entry." The article traced the evolution of the term "social justice warrior" (SJW) back to the early 1990s, where it was sometimes used as a sensationalized way of acknowledging or memorializing notable figures, including musicians, clergy, and filmmakers, who promoted progressive ideals in their fields.

Ohlheiser used Google Trends to understand how and when the term became a pejorative and found that the popularity of the term first picked up in the early days of Gamergate. (A more recent check on the term shows that its peak use occurred in the month leading up to the election of Donald Trump in 2016.)

The use of SJW as an insult gained currency in places like Reddit and 4chan as a derogatory term for feminist and antiracist activists who were mocked and ridiculed for their "delusional" dedication to progressive politics. SJWs were often portrayed in memes as deranged and mentally ill, overweight, ugly, and with attention-grabbing hair colors. SJWs were commonly held by the alt-right to be insincere in their political and social beliefs, angling for reputation over all other concerns. They were fake technologists, and any men who were allies were considered "beta males" or "white knights" trying to win sexual favor.

A 2018 paper by Adrienne L. Massanari and Shira Chess titled "Attack of the 50-foot social justice warrior" analyzed the portrayal of social justice warriors in meme culture as examples of the "monstrous feminine" archetype, akin to myths like the Medusa or the Sirens. (The title recalls the image of the 50-foot-tall Wonder Woman depicted on the **Ms. Magazine** cover of 1972.)

The paper described consistent characteristics of SJWs in chan board memes. They were unappealing according to both feminine or masculine ideals, with exaggerated flaws in their appearance. They were mentally ill, with an obsession for irrelevant or imaginary political crusades. These opponents of the alt-right were depicted as hideous, asexual, mentally diseased, "purple-haired freaks."

In 2016, Milo Yiannopoulos interviewed Open Source Initiative cofounder Eric S Raymond for **Breitbart News** to discuss the "problem" of social justice warriors in open source. Raymond declared that SJWs stood in opposition to hacker values. "I don't care what kind of bigot or what kind of weirdo somebody is when they're not writing code," Raymond stated. "If their code is good, I'll take it." The article quoted another like-minded technologist who agreed that "culture war stuff" had no place in the hacker world, despite the SJW opportunists pushing their agendas into the space.

In spite of the vitriol, some tech justice activists tried to recuperate the term and wear it as an ironic badge of honor. After the headline of a Breitbart attack article referred to me as a "notorious social justice warrior," I decided to adopt the label as part of my professional bio. An artist named Kiva Bay even initiated a project to create pro-SJW trading cards featuring hand-drawn portraits of different activists in the tech justice space.

Model View Culture

We have the technology [...] to produce illusions, involving both belief and knowledge of those beliefs as true, far more complicated than either, by working directly on the brain. What are your social responsibilities when you have a technology like that available?

—Samuel Delany, **Trouble on Triton**

While much of the activism in the tech justice space used Twitter to connect, collaborate, and share the message, there was a need for more nuanced, long-form critiques that wouldn't fit into 140 characters. Blogs were also common and served an important role in the community. But the dialog around social justice in tech was really elevated in January of 2014, with the publication of the first issue of **Model View Culture**.

The online and print magazine was founded as an "independent media platform covering technology, culture and diversity" by tech critic and activist Shanley Kane with artist and designer Amelia Greenhall. Kane edited and produced 43 issues of the magazine from 2014 to 2016, with a brief return to publication in 2020.

MODEL VIEW CULTURE quickly became the intellectual hub for tech feminist, antiracist, and pro-LGBTQ activists online. Hundreds of articles were published on topics ranging from surveillance capitalism to sex tech to Afrofuturism. The magazine gave voice to activists and writers like Jenifer Daniels, Lauren Chief Elk-Young Bear, Sydette Harry, Justine Arrache, and Christina Morillo, as well as giving a platform to dozens of other voices in the movement.

If meme-laden discussion forums were the headquarters of the alt-right, MVC was a hub for progressive politics in tech.

The Changing Face of Tech Conferences

Tech conferences throughout the 2000s were infamous for intense days of talks and intense nights of partying. "Locker-room talk" was used even on stage. Slide presentations with lewd or sexist content intended to be humorous were not uncommon, and there was the endless spectacle of the so-called "booth babes," professional models who were hired to attract attendees to vendor booths.

A culture clash between the old boys' club of the previous generation and the new, more socially aware group of technologists was inevitable.

In 2013, in response to the widespread issue of harassment in these spaces, the annual Python conference PyCon announced the adoption of a code of conduct based on materials created by the Ada Initiative. While PyCon was not alone in adopting such a policy, the idea hadn't really gained a lot of traction yet in the broader conference world.

In February of 2014, Ashe Dryden made a post on Twitter that read: "I will not attend or speak at conferences or other events that do not have a code of conduct." The tweet included the hashtag #CoCPledge. The #CoCPledge message soon picked up momentum.

The idea for the pledge had been circulating among the Python community since late 2012. There was a website called LetsGetLouder. com where people could fill out a form and sign their names to a similar statement. Ashe's tweet brought the cause to a broader audience, starting within the Python and Ruby communities but soon spreading to the broader open source world as well. Over the space of a few days, the hashtag filled with technologists who agreed with the pledge. However, not everyone did.

As the discussion percolated online and offline, a pattern of frequently raised objections about codes of conduct soon emerged. Some people viewed a code of conduct as unnecessary: technologists knew how to treat each other with mutual respect and didn't need to be told how to behave. Some people saw it as pointless: a code of conduct was just "words on paper" that had no purpose except to make people feel better. Some conference organizers worried that adopting an antiharassment policy might lead people to think that there had been problems at the event in the past. And a small but very vocal minority saw codes of conduct as the thin edge of a wedge, part of an invasion of tech by social justice ideas that just didn't belong.

The first argument was, strangely enough, often accompanied by a quote from the 1989 movie **BILL AND TED'S EXCELLENT ADVENTURE**: "be excellent to each other." The sentiment behind this inadvertent meme had even been expressed as early as 1999: the only stated rule for the LinuxChix mailing list was "Be polite. Be helpful. You're bright people. Extrapolate." The website was even more direct: "We don't need a lengthy, detailed rule book because it's all covered by 'be polite, be helpful.'"

In 2014, a regional Chicago tech conference's organizers responded to a question on Twitter about whether that year's event would have a code of conduct, simply with the word "No." Code of conduct advocates were disappointed and angry and, when the organizers refused to engage in conversation, made their feelings clear on Twitter. The conference organizers felt unfairly ganged up on and became defensive. A week or so later, the conference published a short policy statement on their website that reminded attendees of the golden rule ("treat others as you would like to be treated") and ended with the admonition, "We are colleagues, and we treat each other with respect."

Another tech conference in Buffalo, New York, adopted a code of conduct despite protests by the keynote speaker. He closed out the conference by spending his entire talk time rehashing his online arguments, even going so far as to call out and mock members of the audience who had been involved with the effort to normalize codes of conduct.

Toxicity in Open Source

While some critics of codes of conduct at events were open to discussion, despite closely held convictions, those opponents with an anti-social-justice political viewpoint really came out in force later in 2014, when I first published Contributor Covenant.

Conference and meetup codes of conduct were intended to promote equitable and safe treatment of everyone in community spaces. Such spaces were generally short-lived, however. The Contributor Covenant code of conduct brought the same aspirations to where developers spent the majority of their time: in their online open source communities.

Women and other minorities were even less visible in open source than they were in the workplace. According to a 2016 GitHub survey, less than 3% of all open source developers were women. The toxicity of open source communities was certainly a factor. Contributor Covenant set out to change that.

Contributor Covenant opened with a pledge to make the adoptive open source project a "harassment-free environment" and presented a list of protected classes whose safety and well-being would be prioritized. It continued with a set of examples of unacceptable behavior and ended with instructions for reporting a code of conduct violation. The original version of the document was less than 200 words.

An aggressive campaign for broad adoption followed and gained momentum. Soon, Ruby developers could add Contributor Covenant to their projects from the command line with Bundler, the Ruby package manager. In 2016, GitHub even made adopting Contributor Covenant part of its repository creation workflow. Today, Contributor Covenant is used by tens of thousands of open source communities, including nine out of the ten largest open source projects in the world—even Linux.

While codes of conduct at events have become a given and codes of conduct in open source communities are more or less the norm, at the time of their introduction, they were seen as radical and by some as an attempt to pervert the hacker ethic with identity politics.

A vocal contingent felt threatened by the idea that "social justice warriors" were introducing politics into that most sacred of ecosystems, free and open source software. A day after the Linux adoption of Contributor Covenant in 2018, a decision that I had not been involved in or consulted about at all, Kiwi Farms founder Kevin Moon anonymously posted my home address, phone number, and Social Security number on a hijacked and vandalized linux.org website.

I was certainly not alone in being continually doxed and threatened. The alt-right had perfected tactics like doxing, SWATting (inciting police to raid the victim's residence on false evidence), smear campaigns, and death threats during the Gamergate era. And law enforcement had clearly demonstrated their disinterest in treating online harassment as a criminal concern.

The backlash seemed to intensify with each step forward that tech justice advocates made.

Contempt Culture

"I'm a metalogician," Bron said. "I define and redefine the relation between P and Not-P five hours a day, four days a week. Women don't understand.

—Samuel Delany, **TROUBLE ON TRITON**

Whether the alt-right liked it or not, the face of tech was beginning to change. But this new wave of entrants to the field faced significant barriers to entry both in employment and in the open source community. Some of the people who could have been peers or mentors were dismissive or even hostile toward the newcomers.

The new people entering tech didn't yet have the same kinds of experience, clout, or social capital that more established hackers had accumulated. Like many hackers, a lot of these new entrants were self-taught—often having learned HTML, CSS, JavaScript, and PHP to make WordPress sites. But these were programming technologies that were generally considered to be not as serious as languages like C or Java.

There was a long history of gatekeeping in programming, and it became quite fashionable to make fun of programmers who worked in PHP. They were criticized as being the opposite of true hackers, true programmers. Languages like PHP were clearly inferior and therefore so were their practitioners. "At least it's not PHP" was a common refrain whenever someone expressed frustration with their own ("real") programming language.

Programmer Aurynn Shaw saw the connection between these "less serious" languages and the new generation of programmers entering tech, a generation that was markedly more diverse in race, ethnicity, and gender than previous ones had been. Many developers who didn't fit the mold were pushed into front-end jobs that were deemed easier, less demanding, and less important than back-end or full-stack jobs—and then criticized for taking these jobs.

In December of 2015, Shaw published a blog post titled "Contempt Culture." It noted the front-end-vs.-back-end bias that was so widely and sarcastically expressed in venues where programmers gathered, online or offline. The stigma was damaging to gender- and racial-minority candidates who were steered into lower-paying, less prestigious front-end positions, writing the HTML, CSS, and JavaScript that made up the public face of the Internet without enjoying any of the respect that was lavished on their back-end peers. Even today, it's common for developers to mock CSS as inscrutable and any sort of front-end programming languages as lesser tech, without a thought for how this might affect the careers and well-being of equally competent front-end developers.

The autodidactic nature of these new entrants didn't seem to impress many of their peers, and to Shaw, the reason was clear. She reflected that "self-taught narratives" involving hacking WordPress were completely valid, but not "blessed" by the hacker community. Rather, these narratives were looked down upon because they were "a path that is predominately for women."

The Pipeline Problem

Decentralization was one of the first hacker virtues that the new generation adopted and adapted. As the broader business world went all-in on Internet technologies, there was skyrocketing demand for programmers that colleges and universities in the United States simply could not keep up with. What's more, many of the graduates coming out of computer science programs lacked any kind of experience with contemporary engineering practices like pair programming, agile methodology, and test-driven development.

The void was quickly filled by efforts to rapidly train and onboard a new crop of developers to meet demand, and the "learn to code" movement soon took root.

On the business side, this resulted in a boom time for "programming bootcamps," which promised lucrative careers in tech for anyone who could afford time away from employment and family responsibilities for an intensive 12- or 16-week program, often with exorbitant tuition. It was a chance that thousands of would-be programmers were willing to take for their shot at success in the field.

Another set of options available to early entrants came from a wave of (mostly free) progressive training and mentoring programs aimed at new developers from traditionally undervalued or marginalized communities. Programs like Black Girls Code, various language-specific Bridge Foundry initiatives, and RubyTogether's RubyMe mentorship project worked to break down barriers for these new programmers.

The learn-to-code movement was a reaction against centralized education and credentialing, both of which were priced beyond the reach of most aspiring developers. But both bootcamps and targeted training programs only addressed half of the problem, the so-called pipeline problem of getting more people into tech. What happened to them when they got those jobs didn't get the same kind of attention at first.

Giving a Hand Up

I mean, when you have forty or fifty sexes, and twice as many religions, however you arrange them, you're bound to have a place it's fairly easy to have a giggle at. But it's also a pretty pleasant place to live, at least on that level.

—Samuel Delany, **Trouble on Triton**

The hacker virtue around the life-changing potential of computers was strongly embraced. But some of the early breakthroughs that women and minorities were making in the industry had been bittersweet; many of the people who had broken through against all odds found themselves in hostile workplaces with managers and peers who viewed them as different and often somehow lesser. Many startups faced issues with on-the-job sexism, racism, and transphobia and were fundamentally ill-equipped to deal with any sort of personnel challenges like these.

The problem was especially clear to those who had achieved "firsts": being the first female engineer on the team, the first Black developer hired, the first trans employee at the company. They all faced very specific challenges, frustrations, and setbacks from an industry and culture that wasn't designed with their needs in mind and didn't have support and understanding from their mostly male, mostly white managers and coworkers.

Those who had been able to break through barriers to entry in tech wanted to give a hand up to those who were to follow. An active but informal "whisper network" kept marginalized tech workers informed about which companies were (relatively) safe and which ones were problematic. Informal mentorship and outreach on the parts of the "firsts" became the norm for recruiting, retaining, and supporting their similarly marginalized peers in the industry. Those who had achieved some degree of success didn't see workplace aggressions as some sort of hazing ritual; they rightly recognized it as a response to challenges in the status quo around who was allowed to work in tech.

Soon, companies came to recognize the importance of attracting and retaining more diverse employees. Study after study confirmed what many already suspected: diverse teams were more productive and cohesive, and companies with diversity reflected in their C-suite outperformed their monocultural rivals.

While some companies did take the promise and potential of diversifying their workforces seriously, and on ethical grounds, many of the DEI and outreach programs that were springing up across the tech industry were half-hearted at best and even deceptive at worst. And for a lot of those who came in through those programs, a lesson quickly learned was that diversity was not the same as inclusion.

The Epidemic of Imposter Syndrome

Lacking some of the familiar signals of success of their peers from more homogenous backgrounds, the reaction to more diverse technologists entering the workplace was often to question their credentials. Critics of outreach and other DEI efforts took to using the term "diversity hires" to indicate people who they believed were given jobs because of their identities, not their merit. When challenged over discriminatory hiring practices, such critics often complained that they didn't want to "lower the bar" in hiring, implying that "diverse" candidates were less skilled and competent.

It was repeated complaints like these, combined with a lack of recognition by their peers and their bosses, that led to widespread feelings of inadequacy among newcomers to the tech industry. People were reacting to the pervasive feeling that they were held to a different, and constantly shifting, set of standards than their white male colleagues.

Lack of positive feedback combined with a constant feeling of not being welcome led a lot of new technologists, especially those from marginalized backgrounds, to feel like they were never going to be able to meet expectations. They blamed themselves for lack of success and recognition. "Imposter syndrome" became a popular topic at meetups and conferences and on social media.

Lots of efforts were launched to address these disparities through a combination of skill-building and career development. As one example, tech entrepreneur Dr. Kortney Ziegler crowdfunded the Trans*H4CK Project, which organized a series of hackathons bringing together trans and queer technologists and their allies to design and create tools and resources to empower the transgender community. Similar events sprang up all over the world, catering to the needs of different, specific groups, including Black, Latino, queer, female, nonbinary, and other technologists.

A notable example was a conference called Write/Speak/Code, created and organized by a Chicago-based developer named Rebecca Miller-Webster. The event, which ran from 2013 to 2018, was divided into three distinct tracks, focusing on building skills and experience with technical blogging, conference speaking, and software development. The event brought together women and nonbinary technologists of all experience levels, challenging them to "own their expertise" as a tonic against imposter syndrome.

Tech justice advocates had a mature awareness of the intersectional nature of identities and group membership. This was something that Delany had criticized as missing from the progressive activism of earlier eras. In the tech justice advocacy of the 2010s, collaboration and support across social boundaries were encouraged as a norm.

About That Meritocracy of Yours

Such overdetermined systems, hard enough to revise, are even harder to abolish.

—Samuel Delany, **TROUBLE ON TRITON**

In an article about "defending" open source from the threat of the SJWs, alt-right figure Milo Yiannopoulos declared that the strength of open source was that it was both egalitarian and libertarian. He was referring to meritocracy.

But meritocracy was coming under new scrutiny. Its claims of leveling the playing field for equal participation by anyone regardless of race, gender, or other characteristics had, in the real world, fallen far short of its promise. If meritocracy was egalitarian, and only the best coders could rise to the top, how could tech's domination by white men be explained, unless one believed that white men were inherently superior, the very premise of white supremacy?

Tech justice advocates were clear in their critique of meritocracy as a governing principle. One of its critical flaws, at least in the open source context, was that it valued what you produce in place of all other considerations, including who was actually free to participate. People with family or other responsibilities away from the computer didn't have endless hours after working their full-time jobs to hack on open source. Nor did they tend to land the kind of corporate jobs where they were paid to work on it. The system was designed to reward those with the least outside responsibilities and the most free time: the exact demographic that thrived in meritocracy. And with open source participation increasingly being used as a sign of competence by would-be employers, these disparities in who could participate had serious consequences.

Rather than accepting meritocracy as an immutable constant in the field of tech, advocates made the case for addressing the systemic inequities that it reinforced. They imagined a world where it wasn't just your output that was a measure of your worth as a developer. It was also the unique perspectives and lived experiences of moving through the world as an "other" that could inform the work for the better. The classic case of hands-free washroom faucets that couldn't detect Black skin was commonly referenced as an example of what happens when technology is developed in a monoculture: if you don't think to test on Black skin, you're more likely to develop a technology that doesn't work on Black skin. The same applied to the lack of effective content moderation and antiharassment technologies in online spaces: if you had no direct experience of harassment, you'd probably not consider how the feature you were working on could be used as a tool of harassment.

Antisocial Coding

Despite the criticisms, meritocratic idealism persisted and remained the norm in open source spaces, but was also ingrained in corporate culture. It was not unusual for tech companies to promote themselves as having meritocratic cultures, rewarding top performers with raises, bonus benefits, and all-important social status. Some companies went so far as to adopt "flat" organizational philosophies, at least in their software engineering departments.

GitHub was one such company. Its devotion to an idealized meritocracy was evident in an absence of specific job titles, total lack of managers below the C-suite, and the famous circular meritocracy rug in a model White House Oval Office near the lobby of its headquarters in San Francisco. The rug was a parody of the Presidential Seal of the United States and featured the company's "octocat" mascot holding a shield emblazoned with a git branch icon. The text around the seal read "The United Meritocracy of GitHub."

A flat structure with no managers probably seemed like paradise to a lot of its early employees, but the company soon learned a hard lesson about the shortcomings of monoculture, in a controversy that shook the company to its foundations.

Julie Ann Horvath was a feminist and designer who had joined the company in 2012. In addition to her paid work, Horvath organized an all-women talk series called Passion Project, intended to inspire more diverse candidates to work at the company. When cofounder Chris Wanstrath became CEO at the beginning of 2014, Horvath and some of the other employees even convinced him to rethink the meritocratic principles at work in the organization and consider whether that was really the best model. The rug was soon removed.

Despite these early wins, Horvath found herself fighting a culture of aggressive communication, including comments in pull requests, hostile interactions with male coworkers, and finally even harassment from cofounder Tom Preston-Werner and his wife Theresa.

In 2014, Horvath departed the company and soon came forward with allegations against the Preston-Werners that described a pattern of misbehavior and continued ignoring of complaints from Horvath and other employees. The company initially refused to acknowledge Horvath's allegations, but eventually conducted an investigation that determined that the company's cofounder had in fact behaved in an inappropriate and unprofessional manner. Preston-Werner was allowed to resign, and top executives promised to put people and processes in place to deal with similar issues in the future.

Horvath's situation was not unique, but the publicity it garnered brought more attention to the problem of sexism in tech. Following her example, other women and marginalized people working in tech came forward with stories of their own. The tech press reported on the widespread problems with harassment on the job, and even publications outside of the tech world, including the **NEW YORK TIMES**, assigned reporters to write about the issue.

New Ways to Open Source

Everything in a science-fiction novel should be mentioned at least twice (in at least two different contexts).

—Samuel Delany, **TROUBLE ON TRITON**

What happened at GitHub was important not only because of its prominence as a tech company but because of its central position in the world of open source software development. There were plenty of competitors to GitHub, especially in the enterprise space, but the company still maintained a near-monopoly on hosting open source projects globally.

Working in public, with contributions from around the world, and sharing knowledge with the broader community were all important parts of open source culture and reflected the hacker virtues of both hands-on computing and the free flow of information.

The information flowing through open source wasn't all just code. As open source software became more mature and more popular, there were new demands being placed on maintainers. For one thing, there was the dreaded documentation to write: the plague of blank README files had to be addressed. After all, how could you tell someone to RTFM ("read the fucking manual") when there was no FM to R?

New opportunities and ways to contribute soon opened up. Thriving online open source projects attracted communities of adopters and contributors, and those communities needed tending to remain healthy and attract new members. With the increased popularity of web-based applications and developments in cross-platform native UI technologies, there was a new demand for UX and interaction designers in the space.

Most open source projects on GitHub had a file named CONTRIBUTING in their root directories. Typically, this document described the project's procedures for opening and responding to issues and pull requests. But with the emerging understanding that it was not simply code contributions that kept an open source project thriving and competitive, there was a need to define different kinds of roles available to contributors.

Software developer Julia Nguyen provided a shining example of welcoming diverse ways of participating in her if-me.org project. if-me.org was designed as a platform to support individuals, activists, and organizations working in mental health. The project's carefully written CONTRIBUTING file provided detailed descriptions of roles for developers, designers, testers, translators, and technical writers, with comprehensive documentation on how to perform these various roles and what the expectations were for each.

Expanding the possibilities of ways of contributing to open source opened the doors for a lot more people to participate and helped to address some of the issues with homogeneous groups of contributors. But it also fed into the stereotype of new entrants into open source being less technical, and therefore less important, than those who had come before them.

Creative Coding

Rather than being chased away from tech entirely in the face of rampant elitism, new technologists continued to find innovative ways of using code to change their lives and make an impact on the world around them. The hacker virtue of beautiful code attracted artistic programmers and technology-oriented creatives alike to use code to make beautiful things: a movement described as "creative coding."

Creative coding projects combined technology with the arts, often producing surprising, delightful, or poignant pieces that combined the best of both worlds. The movement was the home for curious hackers who didn't quite fit with traditional engineering culture and also didn't quite fit in traditional art culture.

Some of the works that came out of the creative coding movement hearkened back to the early days of computer art, like Grace Hertlein's annual contests in Edmund Berkeley's computing magazine.

One example of an enabling technology for the creative coding movement came in the form of a library and IDE called Processing. Processing was developed in the early 2000s as a tool to teach visual designers how to program, created by Casey Reas and Ben Fry at the MIT Media Lab. Its popularity led to the formation of the nonprofit Processing Foundation, which brought on a diverse board of directors to guide its ongoing mission. Korean-American artist, writer, and musician Johanna Hedva joined the organization as its first Director of Advocacy and is credited with helping to develop the organization's open and diverse culture.

In 2013, the Processing Foundation supported the development of the p5.js project, a port of the Processing environment from Java to JavaScript, which unlocked new possibilities for creative coding for the web.

The 2010s also saw renewed interest in the trend of hands-on electronics projects that had sprung up some years before. Projects like Arduino, with Creative Commons–licensed hardware designs and open source–licensed coding tools, put hardware hacking within reach of artists, musicians, crafters, and other creative individuals, who created projects ranging from glitch art to bizarre musical instruments to complex networks of sensors and displays for art and museum exhibits.

Soon companies like SparkFun, Adafruit, and others were doing a booming business selling miniature circuit boards and components. The Raspberry Pi was released in 2012, putting the power of the Linux operating system (based on the Debian distribution) into tiny but fully functional computers that could be integrated into projects of all kinds. Just as Berkeley's GENIAC kits had encouraged a new generation to explore the fundamentals of computers, the creative coding movement took the hands-on imperative to heart and put computing technology in the hands of people who didn't always fit the mold of what a hacker was supposed to look like.

Reflection

The tech justice movement set out to make the tech world more diverse, welcoming, and inclusive and to support a new generation of hackers eager to use computers and other technologies to change society for the better.

But the timing of the movement, with the simultaneous political shift to the right in world politics and the ongoing "culture war" playing out in popular media, made the struggle more difficult and costly than it otherwise might have been. The rise of the alt-right political movement in the United States coincided with (and fed into) the backlash against the new people and ideas entering the tech sector. Activism in the space was dangerous, and, as we will see, progress often came at a steep price.

CHAPTER 12

An Ambiguous Heterotopia

In his 1962 book **THE STRUCTURE OF SCIENTIFIC REVOLUTIONS**, science historian and philosopher Thomas Kuhn described a sort of ideological gulf that opens periodically in the scientific academy. The establishment and its institutions accrete around a central theme or problem and become experts in it. In time, some practitioners discover a new theme or problem that warrants their attention. This discovery marks a potential paradigm shift (a term coined in Kuhn's book).

There are three possible outcomes with regard to the establishment's reaction. The first involves procrastination, putting off decisions or even discussions of the new paradigm indefinitely. The second is accommodation; the establishment finds a way to adapt itself to the pursuit of the new theme or problem. The third is open conflict, with the risk that existing institutions may find themselves replaced by new institutions under the new paradigm.

The techno-social revolution unfolding throughout the 2010s was no different than the ones that had come before. Existing institutions could either adapt to the new paradigm or be replaced. But procrastination was off the table.

© Coraline Ada Ehmke 2025
C. A. Ehmke, *We Just Build Hammers*, https://doi.org/10.1007/979-8-8688-1249-1_12

Culture As Technology

TROUBLE ON TRITON is set in the year 2112 and apparently in the same universe that we ourselves inhabit. It is implied that the first place beyond Earth that humans settled was Mars. The book does little to distinguish between the cultures of the two planets by the time the action of the story takes place. They are presented more as dangerous relics of the past than any sort of ancestral homeland to the modern human race.

The leap in technology required to settle beyond Mars would be twice as complex as what was required for getting to Mars in the first place. The complexity and maturity of the culture on Triton, and the lingering sense of decay in its architecture, hints at several generations of humans having spent their lives on the moon. This puts its initial colonization sometime late in the mid-twenty-first century. But what had driven the desire to colonize the outer solar system? Were the colonists running *to* something or running *from* something?

It's interesting that Delany never explains either the social catalysts behind the colonization of the gas giant moons nor the technology that made fleeing the Earth possible in the first place. But it is the culture of the diaspora he describes that is the real testament to humanity's achievements. The scientific revolution wasn't the technology that let people from earth land on one of Neptune's moons. The real revolution started when the first people decided to use technology to make new lives for themselves there.

Starving in the Belly of a Whale

Work now was not for pleasure or pride or reward; all those had been abnegated.

—Samuel Delany, **TROUBLE ON TRITON**

The tech giants of today had fully established themselves in positions of unassailable power by the early 2010s. Some of these companies, like Google, Facebook, Twitter, and Amazon in particular, had an outsized impact on the Internet because of the centrality of (and monopolistic holds over) the services they provided: search, advertising, social media, ecommerce, and infrastructure.

It was well understood by leaders in the tech justice movement that bringing about significant change in how the industry dealt with the marginalized, both developers and users, would need to be coordinated across multiple domains: not just in open source but in corporate tech as well. Efforts were made throughout the 2010s to change tech companies from the inside. Progressive engineers could use their positions at companies like these to organize internal efforts to promote diversity and equity.

On the surface, many tech companies seemed to embrace some of the ideals of the tech justice advocates, at least as far as DEI, hiring, and other workplace considerations were concerned. Efforts to adapt these principles inside such companies were largely dependent on extra, unpaid labor by marginalized employees themselves, often without meaningful support from managers or the C-suite. They were implicitly expected to do their engineering jobs and their engineering culture jobs at the same time while only being evaluated and promoted based on the former. Meanwhile, in the workplace, they faced the same toxicity and ingrained systemic problems that they were hired to "fix" in the first place.

Proponents of change, even those specifically hired to solve some of the problems of on-the-job inequity and lack of diversity, often found themselves on very short leashes and under tremendous amounts of scrutiny.

The Glass Cliff Phenomenon

To the extent they will not conform to our ways, there is a subtle swing: the materials of instruction are pulled further away and the materials of destruction are pushed correspondingly closer.

—Samuel Delany, **Trouble on Triton**

A 2013 paper titled "Above the glass ceiling: When are women and racial/ethnic minorities promoted to CEO?," written by researchers Alison Cook and Christy Glass, coined the term "glass cliff" to describe a particular phenomenon that sometimes occurs in response to a company finding itself in some sort of social crisis.

The researchers studied Fortune 500 companies that hired white women or men and women of color as CEOs in the wake of scandal or catastrophe. Such CEOs were set up as saviors who would turn things around and put the company back on course. They noted that in most cases, however, these CEOs had significantly shorter tenures than their white male counterparts and were generally fired before having enough time to oversee any substantive changes. In all cases, the crisis CEOs were immediately replaced with white men. The companies got great PR for their "diversity hire" and a great scapegoat at the same time, before returning to business as usual.

The paper went on to explore the question of why, even when recognizing the glass cliff situation, marginalized people continued to take such high-risk positions. The conclusion that the authors reached was that, for many such candidates, this might be the only chance that they would get for such a high position. They had no choice but to accept levels of risk that would have warned away most of their peers.

Many of the technologists who took jobs within problematic companies or toxic cultures to try to bring about change faced the glass cliff scenario. What's worse, when a well-known tech justice advocate was hired on to one of these companies and seemed to be making progress, it was often taken as a signal to other marginalized technologists that it was becoming a better place for them to work. The presence of a change agent was taken to be a strong signal of safety.

It could be devastating to be wrong. One of the strategies to get better intelligence on these companies was developing a whisper network.

The Whisper Network

An essential conflict within a lot of these companies was the clash between those who benefited most from the status quo and those who sought to reform it. The backlash against change was often brutal, even within the walls of corporations and under the watchful eye of human resources departments. Some engineers, often the "firsts" of their particular demographic at a particular workplace, learned hard lessons about the realities hidden behind certain companies' public commitment to DEI efforts. In many cases, they lacked peers to talk to frankly and confidentially about the issues they faced on the job.

The revolution in social media created webs of connections between leading figures in the tech justice movement, activists working on the issues inside tech companies, and job seekers who wanted to know what they were getting into before applying. An informal network (or, more precisely, a decentralized network of networks) formed almost organically. The network existed to share group intelligence about specific companies, specific executives, and specific bad actors that should be avoided by marginalized technologists looking for their next job. It was dubbed the "whisper network."

There was no structure or common medium for the information that traveled across the whisper network. Sometimes, information would be collected on a secret Google Sheets spreadsheet for anyone to update and read; sometimes, there were dedicated channels in group chat apps for asking for advice; and sometimes, information was simply spread by word of mouth.

Whisper networks were not a new invention and had been around for decades in the entertainment, music, and sex work industries. The adaptation of the concept into the tech justice space, including lessons learned about such lists becoming public, served as a valuable tool for helping marginalized technologists navigate the minefield of the tech industry.

A common criticism of whisper networks was one of accessibility. The richer your social graph, the more whispers you were likely to hear. New entrants to the tech space might not yet know the right people to ask or have the same access to community intelligence as their more seasoned counterparts. Several attempts were made to centralize reports of harassment and abuse to address the findability problem, but these were plagued by technical, social, ethical, and legal challenges.

The most successful attempt to document abuses within the tech industry more broadly was the "Timeline of Incidents" page on the Geek Feminism Wiki, compiling events dating back to the 1960s but focusing on incidents of harassment, abuse, and assault from the 2010s. Unlike most public whisper network lists, the names of specific people were not redacted from the wiki. But the Geek Feminism Wiki was hosted on a public platform provider's site, subject to constant brigading and hampered by lack of antiharassment features. Eventually, the wiki was locked and archived.

Despite their numerous shortcomings, whisper networks played a vital role not only in safety but in helping victims of workplace harassment know that they were not alone. You could find solidarity in whispers.

Hush Clauses

Some of the people who had been hired into roles at tech companies to bring about change from inside found it impossible to do their jobs. Confrontations and clashes with change-resistant layers of management often led to firings. Once companies started realizing the reputation cost of firings like these, it became common practice for severance packages to be predicated on signing a legal agreement to not talk about the details of their employment or dismissal.

These were so-called "hush clauses," more properly known as "nondisparagement agreements." These legal instruments force someone to sign away the rights to their story with the severance they were owed being held hostage. Although of dubious value in court, it was both legally risky to test and often economically risky to forego the severance money.

Hush clauses were common enough by the mid-2010s that the tech press was starting to pay attention. Numerous women were interviewed, often anonymously, for articles on the phenomenon. Panels were organized. Blog posts were published. Conference talks were given. But for a while, nothing really changed.

Hush clauses remained a go-to tool used by tech companies with spotty records to preserve their reputations as good places to work. Demand for software developers remained high, and workplaces were in high-stakes competition with one another to attract talent. Reputation was everything.

The Whistleblowers

Hush clauses were not always effective deterrents. Conflict between equity-minded technologists and the companies they worked for sometimes called for airing grievances in public. Frustrated employees could become whistleblowers when they found themselves unable to bring about change from the inside like they were led to believe.

In 2020, Pinterest employees Ifeoma Ozoma and Aerica Shimizu Banks quit the company, citing pushback on their efforts to address internal issues including disparities in pay and racism within the company. Ozoma had previously made a name for herself as an advocate for fighting medical disinformation on the platform. Following her exit from Pinterest, Ozoma worked to pass the Silenced No More Act in California, legislation that offered protection to whistleblowers in issues of discrimination regardless of nondisclosure agreements or hush clauses.

Google engineer Timnit Gebru was one of the AI researchers who, in 2019, signed a petition for Amazon to cease sales of facial recognition technology to law enforcement agencies. Noting algorithmic bias against people of color, Gebru insisted that the technology was too dangerous to be used. Gebru would leave Google a year later amid a controversy over a paper on the risks of large language models such as those being used at Google. Gebru then founded the independent Distributed Artificial Intelligence Research Institute (DAIR) to study the effects of AI on marginalized groups.

Tech workers across the industry were also beginning to organize around their companies' contracts with law enforcement, the military, and, increasingly, the Border Patrol and the Immigration and Customs Enforcement Agency (ICE).

FOSS's Human Rights Crisis

Suffering the wound of having wounded, he thought: Help me.

—Samuel Delany, **Trouble on Triton**

In 2019, at the height of the immigration and human rights crisis at the southern border of the United States, a nationwide social media campaign was being conducted to draw attention to the complicity of tech companies in what was happening at the border under the authority of ICE. The campaign was organized by the Latinx activist group Mijente, using the "#NoTechForICE" hashtag.

One of the companies called out for its ICE contracts in the #NoTechForICE tweets was Chef, which made open source software for cloud server configuration and management. Seth Vargo, a former Chef employee and creator of several open source tools in the Chef ecosystem, saw a retweet of the Mijente post. He was horrified to think that software he had written was being used in connection with human rights abuses.

Vargo reacted from a place of conscience. He removed his source code from GitHub and pulled his libraries from the RubyGems repository. Server deployments around the world started failing, as many of the libraries that Vargo had deleted were dependencies in other companies' Chef configurations. Chef intervened with GitHub and RubyGems, asserting ownership and authority over the code. Their argument was that, despite it being authored by Vargo and released as open source, it was written while he was employed by Chef. Within the space of two hours, Vargo's software was restored.

He was acting on his sincerely held convictions: that his open source code should not be used for harm. But the Open Source Definition explicitly states (in its annotations) that code must be free for use for any purpose, "even explicitly 'evil' purposes." The open source establishment not only didn't support Vargo's actions from a legal perspective, they were also philosophically opposed to it.

Vargo updated the README.md file in his original repository to read, "I have a moral and ethical obligation to prevent my source from being used for evil."

Ethics in the Open

In reaction to the story of Vargo's dilemma, there was a general outcry among a number of ethically minded technologists in open source. There was a lot of frustration over how the situation was handled between Chef, GitHub, and RubyGems. And there was outrage over the hard "open source is neutral" stance taken by open source traditionalists.

In response, I sat down with a text editor and pasted the text of the MIT license into a fresh file. With some help from a trusted colleague, I added the following clause to the stock MIT license:

> *The software may not be used by individuals, corporations, governments, or other groups for systems or activities that actively and knowingly endanger, harm, or otherwise threaten the physical, mental, economic, or general well-being of individuals or groups in violation of the United Nations Universal Declaration of Human Rights.*

I titled the modified license the "Hippocratic License," set up a quick static site at firstdonoharm.dev, and created a firestorm in the open source community.

Bruce Perens, author of the Open Source Definition, responded the next day in a blog post titled "Sorry, Ms Ehmke, The Hippocratic License Can't Work." He applauded the sentiment but insisted that copyright was not the right vehicle for enforcing human rights. What's more, he wrote, ethics are slippery and change "from place to place and person to person." This was the classic "Argument of the Beard": he was asserting that, because of the existence of a gray area in ethics, there could be no clear right or wrong. This was a point that Berkeley had handily refuted decades earlier.

Eric S Raymond took the criticism much further, launching into a series of profanity-laden complaints and vitriolic personal attacks directed at me. His behavior actually resulted in Raymond, a cofounder of the organization, being banned from the Open Source Initiative's "license-discuss" listserv for code of conduct violations.

The controversy was what was needed at the time, and in fact, sparking controversy was the point of releasing the Hippocratic License in the first place. The objective was to draw the discussion of the meaning of open source beyond the OSI's laser focus on licenses. It was a question about the ethical responsibility of open source software developers for the way that their creations were used in the real world. As such, it was a callback to Edmund Berkeley's lifelong campaign for ethics in computing.

The Hippocratic License acted as a lightning rod for conversation and for raising questions about whether the Open Source Definition, and the open source establishment itself, was up to the challenge of dealing with the complex techno-social conflicts unfolding around the world.

Soon, a small group of ethics-minded open source activists came together to announce the launch of the Ethical Source Movement. The movement was incorporated as the Organization for Ethical Source and has gained legal recognition of nonprofit status in the United States. OES's mission is to leverage open source technology for justice and equity, advocate for human rights in the digital landscape, and make participation in online communities more inclusive.

Since its founding, the organization has released two fully revamped, legally drafted versions of the Hippocratic License. It's also taken on stewardship of the Contributor Covenant code of conduct and is engaged in research and development of new tools for equitable governance in open source and other digital communities.

Mozilla Embraces Cultural Change

Everything in a science-fiction novel should be mentioned at least twice (in at least two different contexts).

—Samuel Delany, *Trouble on Triton*

As Kuhn predicted, new institutions were emerging to challenge the dominant culture exemplified by the tech giants and open source traditionalists alike. Where organizations resisted change, change found expression in new organizations.

But not all institutions were so resistant to change. In the open source world, Mozilla had long embraced the cultural and techno-social changes that were taking place in the industry. Mozilla famously tilted the power balance on the web away from Microsoft and toward open source back in 1998 and managed to stay true to its mission while evolving its strategies toward ensuring the Internet was used to promote social good.

The original Mozilla Manifesto, penned in 2007, codified the ethical framework that the organization aspired to. The Manifesto listed ten principles, ranging from declaring the Internet a global public good, to advocating for privacy, to the benefits of free and open source and the need for balance between commercial pursuits and public interest. It was powerful but not controversial.

Throughout the 2010s, Mozilla managed an impressive technology portfolio that included its Firefox web browser, the Bugzilla issue tracking system, and the email client Thunderbird. But on top of the technical side of open source citizenship, Mozilla also embraced the notion of open source for social good.

In 2017, Mitchell Baker was serving as Mozilla's interim CEO. To mark the tenth anniversary of the Mozilla Manifesto, which she had written, Baker created an addendum she called "Pledge for a Healthy Internet."

Its preamble set the tone, reinforcing the Internet's vast potential as a force for good. But it acknowledged that in recent years, the Internet had also been the vehicle for hate, violence, and disinformation.

In response, the Pledge introduced four new principles to the Mozilla Manifesto. Quoting:

- We are committed to an internet that includes all the peoples of the earth—where a person's demographic characteristics do not determine their online access, opportunities, or quality of experience.

- We are committed to an internet that promotes civil discourse, human dignity, and individual expression.

- We are committed to an internet that elevates critical thinking, reasoned argument, shared knowledge, and verifiable facts.

- We are committed to an internet that catalyzes collaboration among diverse communities working together for the common good.

Journalist David Pierce interviewed Baker for **PROTOCOL** in 2020. When he asked her why she had revisited the Manifesto and written the Pledge, she responded, "I'm not spending my life building an open system that's good for trolls and surveillance organizations and violent groups."

At the time of its publication in 2017, there was a very loud, very negative response to the Healthy Internet Pledge by a small number of vocal critics. These were a minority of people in tech who saw the Pledge as further evidence that open source was being overrun by social justice warriors, and even revered institutions were being pressured into embracing progressive politics.

Nevertheless, Mozilla continued to work for a more equitable internet, spending the next several years focusing on issues like Internet ethics, user privacy, and the problem of disinformation.

Losing Twitter

Our society in the Satellites extends to its Earth and Mars emi-grants, at the same time it extends instruction on how to con-form, the materials with which to destroy themselves both psychologically and physically all under the same label: Freedom.

—Samuel Delany, **TROUBLE ON TRITON**

Activists inside and outside of tech had learned over the past decade how to make effective use of social media. They had developed strategies for essentially hacking the big platforms to turn them into tools for planning, organizing, and getting the message out in resistance to the country's political and cultural shift to the right.

In 2020, following the murder of George Floyd at the hands of a Minneapolis police officer, massive antiracist protests sprung up across the United States. The #BlackLivesMatter hashtag, which had been in use since 2013, gained new life and was used as a way of mobilizing and supporting the protestors. The resulting protest movement was the largest demonstration of the power of technology for activism that the United States had ever seen.

Part of the backlash against the movement involved dismantling social media as it had existed, removing it from the activists' toolkit. With the acquisition and reinvention of Twitter as X following Elon Musk's takeover of the company in 2022, even the meager protections that the platform had previously offered were quickly stripped away.

Twitter had been as useful as it had been toxic to organizers and activists. But now the entire Trust & Safety team at the company had been fired; policies promoting free speech above all other concerns were put into place; rules around hateful speech and conduct were relaxed. The company fell into conflict with governments around the world, including the United States and Australia, over some of these new policies.

While casual social media users either didn't notice or care or perhaps migrated to platforms like Instagram and TikTok, many technologists took refuge on Mastodon. (Mastodon has the distinction of being open source software for social media; it also has the distinction of being the backbone technology for Donald Trump's "Truth Social" network.)

Mastodon didn't have the same activist culture as Twitter did, especially Twitter at the height of the tech justice movement days. The same algorithmic virality that powered hate campaigns on Twitter had also been put to use by activists to respond, organize, and broadcast. The way that Mastodon was architected deliberately resisted this kind of viral transmission.

But Mastodon was also architected for federation and decentralization. These characteristics meant that activists had access to better safety tools and were no longer reliant on a central, commercial entity, or its billionaire owner's whims, in exchange for access.

Decentralized Everything

The decentralization of social media promised by tools like Mastodon is part of a larger decentralization movement. There are calls to return to self-published websites, reviving the so-called "small web." As search engines yield final authority to AI, hand-curated Internet directories are starting to make a comeback. We're even seeing the only-semi-ironic return of webrings. Once again, hackers are organizing to save the Internet.

In 2019, the Internet Archive coalesced several years of meetups, conferences, and conversations into an effort called DWeb, for "distributed web." DWeb was established with the mission to connect "the people, projects and protocols essential to building a decentralized web. A web that is more private, reliable, secure and open. A web with many winners—returning to the original vision of the World Wide Web and internet."

The DWeb principles recall the progressive ideals of Mozilla's "Pledge for a Healthy Internet." They are

1. Technology for human agency

2. Distributed benefits

3. Mutual respect

4. Humanity

5. Ecological awareness

A distributed web, on a decentralized internet, would mean that movements would no longer be beholden to big tech platforms for their communication and infrastructure. The Internet would finally fulfill the hacker ideal of decentralization of power in service of the underdog.

We're Seeing Other People

You know, the human race has done more real, honest to goodness evolving since the beginning of the twentieth century than probably at any other time in the previous ten thousand years.

—Samuel Delany, **Trouble on Triton**

Despite the near-continuous, sometimes even violent backlash against promoting ideals like equity in tech, some gains have still been made, and these are worth noting.

The demographic changes in the open source world were certainly the result of the work of hundreds of women and other marginalized technologists to promote the ideals diversity and inclusivity in their communities.

In a 2002 report published by the International Institute for Infonomics titled "Free/Libre and Open Source Software: Survey and Study," there is included a "Survey of Developers" that provides a glimpse of how diverse

FOSS was at the turn of the century. The section on gender in the summary concluded that "women do not play a role in the development of Open Source and Free Software; only 1.1% of the FLOSS sample is female."

According to more recent research, for example, that published in the 2022 paper "Women's Participation in Open Source Software: A Survey of the Literature," around 10% of GitHub users today are women, and they produce about 5% of all pull requests. Of the most active accounts on GitHub, nearly 7% of them belong to women. Women also made gains in serving on core teams in more open source projects.

In 2002, at a meetup of open source enthusiasts, there would have been (statistically speaking) one or zero women present. Twenty years later, there would be ten. Ten is not enough and is far from representative or equitable, but it's still ten times as many women as in the previous generation.

In contrast to activist-led efforts to promote diversity, corporate DEI programs have not fared so well. There is not nearly as much growth in the number of women or Black and brown technologists within tech companies themselves.

In a 2021 story for NBC News, April Glaser and Char Adams reported that, despite being the first of the tech giants to publish an annual diversity report, key diversity metrics at Google only moved by a percentage point or less across Black hires, despite the hundreds of millions of dollars nominally spent to address the issues. The same story played out across other large tech companies, from Apple to Facebook. Overall, the percentage of women working in technical positions remained stagnant over two decades at roughly 25–30% of the workforce.

By the early 2020s, fewer companies published their diversity reports at all. Even the Stack Overflow User Survey (often used as a proxy as the only available annual source of data on software developers, however flawed) stopped asking any demographic questions at all besides age as of 2023.

Once again, the open source world might be a beacon of hope. On the African continent, open source communities in Kenya, Nigeria, and Ghana are growing more quickly than anywhere else in the world. There is steady growth in open source participation by technologists from South Asia and East Asia. Developers in South America, Brazil in particular, are gaining ground in terms of the percentage of overall open source contributions. New Zealand is emerging as a surprising tech hub. The open source world is starting to look different and to reflect experiences, values, and aspirations beyond the Californian ideology.

The Changing Meaning of Open

There are many other areas where the open source world has improved since the early 2010s.

We've expanded how we think about the ways of participating in open source. Although there remains an air of elitism among some developers, contributions from people writing documentation, designing interfaces, and triaging bugs are better recognized and acknowledged than they had been.

As the transition in mindset from "open source project" to "open source community" has continued to play out, things like codes of conduct and dedicated community management resources are increasingly the norm.

Following the adoption of explicit social norms came a focus on the importance of governance as well. We're seeing the end of the era of the Benevolent Dictator for Life, as open source grows too critical to the world to be left in the hands of a few strong personalities.

Open source itself has been hacked and, in the true hacker spirit, improved in the process.

Reflection

The final possible outcome in Kuhn's map of scientific revolutions is the splitting off of proponents of change from their more conservative institutions.

In creating new institutions, forming new types of communities, and exploring new spaces for collaboration and organizing, the tech justice movement has moved us closer to the heterotopian ideal. Creating places of difference, and networking them together across technical, geographical, and cultural boundaries, is a solid strategy for opening the way to alternative futures based on social responsibility and the promotion of broad social good.

The technological underpinnings of the heterotopia that Delany portrayed on that Neptunian moon required an entire branch of logic and mathematics to function and was still largely too complex for anyone to understand in its entirety. The modular calculus's complexity came about by using rationality to model the irrationality of human society.

Outside the world of fiction, developing an ethical techno-social foundation for our own world also involves solving some of the most difficult problems we've faced as a society.

But luckily, as technologists of today often brag, we love solving hard problems.

CHAPTER 13

Has the Future Been Written?

The weaving of mankind into one community does not imply the creation of a homogeneous community, but rather the reverse; the welcome and adequate utilization of distinctive quality in an atmosphere of understanding ... Communities all to one pattern, like boxes of toy soldiers, are things of the past, rather than of the future.

—H.G. Wells, *The Outline of History*

Who are the storytellers of our new tomorrows? Who is weaving inspirational or cautionary tales about the future conflicts at the intersection of technology and society? Who are the next generation of scientists, engineers, hackers, and tech activists who will take their lessons and warnings to heart? And what will be the consequences?

Comparing and contrasting the speculative tomorrows described in the previous chapters, what lessons can we take from both warnings against an impending technology-fueled dystopia and visions of how technology can help shape a more equitable world?

Will we learn from the experience of Leo Szilard, who tried to save the world from the atomic bomb that he helped develop?

Will we take Edmund Berkeley's admonitions to heart and accept our larger-than-average share of responsibility to society?

© Coraline Ada Ehmke 2025
C. A. Ehmke, *We Just Build Hammers*, https://doi.org/10.1007/979-8-8688-1249-1_13

Will we continue to evolve the hacker ethic and resist corporate takeover of the Internet, in our pursuit of open and equitable access to technology for everyone?

Will we find a way for our digital societies to be places where we flourish because of our differences, not in spite of them?

H.G. Wells asked the question, "If this one thing were true, what would life be like?" Ask yourself, what is the one thing that you would like to be true, and how would that change your life—and the lives of those around you—for the better? And if you think that it's impossible, take a page from Samuel Delany and ask, "What would have to happen to make this impossible thing possible?"

How can you use both your technical skills and your empathy to help bring that future about? Are you content to keep building "hammers" or "neutral" tech, or are you ready to build a future where technology and society evolve and thrive together?

References and Further Reading

Chapter 1

1. Library of Congress. (n.d.). Immigration to the United States, 1851–1900. Retrieved from https://www.loc.gov/classroom-materials/united-states-history-primary-source-timeline/rise-of-industrial-america-1876-1900/immigration-to-united-states-1851-1900/

2. De Gruyter. (n.d.). Document. Retrieved from https://www.degruyter.com/document/doi/10.1515/9783110806144-011/html

3. BBC Archive. (n.d.). Communications 1922–1932 – H.G. Wells. Retrieved from https://www.bbc.co.uk/archive/communications-1922-1932--hg-wells/z4f6kmn

4. Hines, A. (2020). When did it start? Origin of the foresight field. *World Futures Review*. Retrieved from https://journals.sagepub.com/doi/pdf/10.1177/1946756719889053

5. Gunn, J. (n.d.). *The Science of Science Fiction Writing.*

Chapter 2

1. Lanouette, W. (n.d.). *Genius in the Shadows: A Biography of Leo Szilard, the Man Behind the Bomb.*

2. Hargittai, I., & Hargittai, B. (n.d.). *Wisdom of the Martians of Science: In Their Own Words with Commentaries.*

3. Atomic Heritage Foundation. (n.d.). *The Manhattan Project: An Interactive History.* Retrieved from https://web.archive.org/web/20110612002211/http://www.atomicheritage.org/index.php?option=com_content&task=view&id=392

4. Szilard, L. (1949). My trial as a war criminal. University of Chicago Law Review, 17(1), Article 4. Retrieved from https://chicagounbound.uchicago.edu/uclrev/vol17/iss1/4

5. Rhéaume, C. (2008). Western Scientists' Reactions to Andrei Sakharov's Human Rights Struggle in the Soviet Union, 1968–1989. Human Rights Quarterly, 30(1), 1–20. http://www.jstor.org/stable/20486694

6. Hargittai, B., & Hargittai, I. (2016). Wisdom of the Martians of Science: In their own words with commentaries. Saint Francis University and Budapest University of Technology and Economics. https://doi.org/10.1142/9809

7. Capria, M. M. (2005). Physics before and after Einstein. *IOS Press.*

8. Rhodes, R. (1986). *The Making of the Atomic Bomb.* Simon and Schuster.

9. Voices of the Manhattan Project. (n.d.). Leone Marshall Libby interview. Retrieved from `https://ahf.nuclearmuseum.org/voices/oral-histories/leona-marshall-libbys-interview/`

10. Weart, S., & Weiss Szilard, G. (Eds.). (1978). *Leo Szilard: His Version of the Facts.* Cambridge, Mass.: MIT Press.

11. Groves, L. R. (1962). *Now it Can Be Told: The Story of the Manhattan Project.* New York: Harper & Brothers.

12. Szilard, L. (1964). Szilard's Ten Commandments with introduction by Trude. *Coronado Journal.* Retrieved from `https://library.ucsd.edu/dc/object/bb3516979c`

Chapter 3

1. Stoff, M. B., Fanton, J. F., & Williams, R. H. (Eds.). (1991). *The Manhattan Project: A Documentary Introduction to the Atomic Age.* Temple University Press.

2. Hawkins, H. S., Greb, G. A., & Weiss Szilard, G. (Eds.). (1987). *Toward a Livable World: Leo Szilard and the Crusade for Nuclear Arms Control.* MIT Press.

3. Dannen, G. (2015, January 26). A physicist's lost love: Leo Szilard and Gerda Philipsborn. Retrieved from www.dannen.com/lostlove/

Chapter 5

1. Longo, B. (2013, October 13). On the Procrustean bed: Edmund Berkeley and the social responsibility of computer people.

Chapter 6

1. Berkeley, Edmund Callis. Giant Brains, or, Machines That Think (Classics To Go) (p. 304). Otbebookpublishing. Kindle Edition.

Chapter 7

1. Jaynes, J. (n.d.). *The Origin of Consciousness in the Breakdown of the Bicameral Mind.*

2. The Guardian. (2004, November 4). Retrieved from https://www.theguardian.com/technology/2004/nov/04/onlinesupplement

3. Vanity Fair. (2017, June). Retrieved from https://www.vanityfair.com/news/2017/06/neal-stephenson-metaverse-snow-crash-silicon-valley-virtual-reality

4. Reason. (2005, February 1). Neal Stephenson's past, present, and future. Retrieved from https://reason.com/2005/02/01/neal-stephensons-pastpresent-a

5. Finn, E., & Cramer, K. (Eds.). (n.d.). *Hieroglyph: Stories & Visions for a Better Future.* HarperCollins.

Chapter 8

1. Levy, S. (n.d.). *Hackers: Heroes of the Computer Revolution - 25th Anniversary Edition.* O'Reilly Media.

2. Steinmetz, K. F. (n.d.). *Hacked: A Radical Approach to Hacker Culture and Crime.*

Chapter 9

1. Kirkpatrick, G. (2002). The hacker ethic and the spirit of the information age. *Max Weber Studies*, 2(2), 163–185. Retrieved from http://www.jstor.org/stable/24579606

2. Widder, D. G., Nafus, D., Dabbish, L., & Herbsleb, J. (n.d.). Limits and possibilities for "ethical AI" in open source: A study of deepfakes. Retrieved from https://dl.acm.org/doi/abs/10.1145/3531146.3533779

3. Himanen, P. (2001). *The Hacker Ethic and the Spirit of the Information Age.* Random House.

Chapter 10

1. Matsuuchi, A. (2017). Wonder Woman wears pants: Wonder Woman, feminism and the 1972 "Women's Lib" issue. *Monash University*. Retrieved from https://doi.org/10.4225/03/592280b6ef43d

2. Snorton, C. R. (2014). An ambiguous heterotopia: On the past of black studies' future. *The Black Scholar, 44*(2), 29–36. Retrieved from http://www.jstor.org/stable/10.5816/blackscholar.44.2.0029

3. Delany, S. (1999). *Shorter Views: Queer Thoughts & The Politics of the Paraliterary*. Wesleyan.

4. Dery, M. (1994). *Flame Wars: The Discourse of Cyberculture*. Duke University Press. Retrieved from https://doi.org/10.1215/9780822396765

Chapter 11

1. Massanari, A. L., & Chess, S. (2018). Attack of the 50-foot social justice warrior: The discursive construction of SJW memes as the monstrous feminine. *Feminist Media Studies, 18*(4), 525–542. https://doi.org/10.1080/14680777.2018.1447333

Chapter 12

1. Trinkenreich, B., Wiese, I., Sarma, A., Gerosa, M., & Steinmacher, I. (2022). Women's participation in open source software: A survey of the literature. *ACM Transactions on Software Engineering and Methodology, 31*(4), 81. https://doi.org/10.1145/3510460

2. Frluckaj, H., Dabbish, L., Widder, D. G., Qiu, H. S., & Herbsleb, J. D. (2022). Gender and participation in open source software development. *Proceedings of the ACM on Human-Computer Interaction, 6*(CSCW2), 299. https://doi.org/10.1145/3555190

3. Lee, A., & Carver, J. C. (2019). FLOSS participants' perceptions about gender and inclusiveness: A survey. *Proceedings of the 41st International Conference on Software Engineering (ICSE '19).* IEEE Press, 677–687. https://doi.org/10.1109/ICSE.2019.00077

4. Nafus, D. (2012). "Patches don't have gender": What is not open in open source software. *New Media & Society, 14*(4), 669–683. https://doi.org/10.1177/1461444811422887

5. Vasilescu, B., Capiluppi, A., & Serebrenik, A. (2012). Gender, representation and online participation: A quantitative study of StackOverflow. *2012 International Conference on Social Informatics.* Alexandria, VA, USA, 332–338. https://doi.org/10.1109/SocialInformatics.2012.81

6. Ghosh, R., Glott, A., Krieger, B., & Robles, B. (2002). Free/libre and open source software: Survey and study, part IV: Survey of developers. *International Institute of Infometrics/Merit.*

7. Statista. (n.d.). U.S. women computer workers by ethnicity. Retrieved from https://www.statista.com/statistics/311967/us-women-computer-workers-ethnicity/

8. Geek Feminism. (n.d.). Timeline of incidents. Retrieved from https://web.archive.org/web/20240513153741/https://geekfeminism.fandom.com/wiki/Timeline_of_incidents

9. Cook, A., & Glass, C. (2014). Above the glass ceiling: When are women and racial/ethnic minorities promoted to CEO?. *Strategic Management Journal, 35*, 1080–1089. https://doi.org/10.1002/smj.2161

10. Protocol. (2020, June 15). Mozilla plan to fix internet privacy. Retrieved from https://web.archive.org/web/20200615063741/https://www.protocol.com/mozilla-plan-fix-internet-privacy

11. Mozilla. (n.d.). Mozilla manifesto. Retrieved from https://www.mozilla.org/en-US/about/manifesto/

12. Perens, B. (2019, September 23). Sorry, Ms. Ehmke: The Hippocratic License can't work. Retrieved from http://perens.com/2019/09/23/sorry-ms-ehmke-the-hippocratic-license-cant-work/

Index

A

Adafruit, 224
Afrofuturism, 188
Aiken, Howard, 90, 93
Alsos Mission, 45
Alt-right political movement, 203, 205, 224
Arazi, Ebram, 96
Arduino, 223
Argument of the Beard, 113, 234
Arrache, Justine, 209
Ashby, Madeline, 137
Association for Computing Machinery (ACM), 93, 94, 115, 129
Atomic energy, 21, 40
    fission, 38
    neutron chain reaction, 3, 34, 35
Atomic weaponry, 21, 39
    Advisory Committee on Uranium, 45, 46
    decision to drop bomb, 52, 53
    Franck report, 54
    Interim Committee, 52
    Manhattan project, 47–49
    Martians, 45
    Szilard petition, 54, 55
    Uranium Club, 44

B

Babel-17, 131
Baker, Mitchell, 236
Banks, Aerica Shimizu, 232
Bay, Kiva, 208
Benevolent Dictator for Life (BDFL), 162, 242
Berkeley, Edmund, 87, 90, 98, 103, 114, 118, 159, 224, 245
    activism, 74
    civilian life, 91
    home computers, 100
    small robots, 100
    in wartime, 90
Bicameral mind, 131, 147
Black Girls Code, 215
#BlackLivesMatter, 238
Bootcamps, 215
Brains Trust, 9
Bridge Foundry, 215
Browser Wars, 155
Bulletin of the Atomic Scientist, 58, 94

Printed in the United States
by Baker & Taylor Publisher Services